MW01035649

LATASHA N. NEVADA DIGGS

VILLAGE

VILLAGE

LATASHA N. NEVADA DIGGS

COFFEE HOUSE PRESS
Minneapolis
2023

"Mother (original by Nagase Kiyoko)" by Kenneth Rexroth, from *Women Poets of Japan*, copyright © 1977 by Kenneth Rexroth and Ikuko Atsumi. Reprinted by permission of New Directions Publishing Corp.

Coffee House Press books are available to the trade through our primary distributor, Consortium Book Sales & Distribution, cbsd.com or (800) 283-3572. For personal orders, catalogs, or other information, write to info@coffeehousepress.org.

Coffee House Press is a nonprofit literary publishing house. Support from private foundations, corporate giving programs, government programs, and generous individuals helps make the publication of our books possible. We gratefully acknowledge their support in detail in the back of this book.

LIBRARY OF CONGRESS CATALOGING-IN-PUBLICATION DATA

Names: Diggs, LaTasha N. Nevada, author.
Title: Village / LaTasha N. Nevada Diggs.
Description: Minneapolis : Coffee House Press, 2023.
Identifiers: LCCN 2022036006 (print) | LCCN 2022036007 (ebook) |
    ISBN 9781566896610 (paperback) | ISBN 9781566896627 (epub)
Subjects: LCGFT: Poetry.
Classification: LCC PS3604.I394 V55 2023 (print) | LCC PS3604.I394 (ebook) |
    DDC 811/.6—dc23/eng/20221012
LC record available at https://lccn.loc.gov/2022036006
LC ebook record available at https://lccn.loc.gov/2022036007

PRINTED IN THE UNITED STATES OF AMERICA

30 29 28 27 26 25 24 23   1 2 3 4 5 6 7 8

for
Gem
Haile
Niya
Nyrel
Jamila
Marion

contents

pan's labyrinth

the magic garden

where are your bones

mother

She is like a cherished, bitter dream,
My nerves cannot forget
Even after I awake.
She prevents all freedom of movement.
If I move, she quickly breaks,
And the splinters stab me.

—Nagase Kiyoko, *Women Poets of Japan*
Translated by Kenneth Rexroth and Ikuko Atsumi

VILLAGE

distillery

Performance

To assist my survivors in making arrangements
at the time of my departure,
i provide the following information:

1.

NOTIFICATION.

i desire that "my peoples,"
of flighty species — two legged, winged, w/ domestic
& international country codes &/or zip codes —
be contacted immediately in order to offer assistance
& relief for any milonga thrown by surviving
estranged blood relatives.

i disinherit all trifling estranged blood relatives.

2.

FUNERAL HOME/DIRECTOR.

i desire that no funeral be held; instead,
M___ V___, T____ T_____, my peoples
winged, w/out scales, w/ capricious international
country codes have been consulted
in customizing a bedazzled urn
& w/ making the celebratory, lampooning roast arrangements
requested in this document.
The arrangements have been made
& are attached to this document as Exhibit 1.

twilight lore

somehow :: my great-aunt Mary Lightfoot erased herself
                    the moment she collapsed on stage

an opera w/ no recording :: no Van Vechten or
    Van Der Zee receipt

what evidence :: if any left available :: concerning
misspellings :: aliases :: contralto or mezzo :: coherent or intoxicated

the surnames & clans i am bound to
as they say :: you mommy :: took to the grave :: we became mythologies

    H over T bordered by an incomplete F

hopscotch over a dress wearing T

        an imbalanced scale tittering in I
        the T died during Double Dutch :: the L resurrects

boxed as an unequal :: put it on a heel & heal, won't you
           but why the Y died?

profile the tribe that liquor built :: its window the sheen of Wild Irish Rose
Night Train bottleneck clunk :: fender bender ascensión conceptual

    now Hammond won't you

make it a brownstone on St. Nicholas :: make it gangrene on the brain
make it an arm amputated :: an estranged first born ::

      a grandson :: prisoner #291865

make it a cell at Allendale Correctional Facility

bonds denied & in denial

or the mind your beeswax's from a bitter, gay grandson :: the rapist's ayotli

or the grandson deported to Panama, compliments of Obama

scooped up by missionaries

worn down by a buzz :: by HIV :: high & numbing

or a walk-up near 7th :: inside a largely vacant tenement
under "Eastern European" ownership

the flash flood rains outside your door

tetanus from flat head nails :: ruined goodies

the Y died :: ladybugs suck salt from a crack in your ceiling
the former walls now beams expose the bruise

divide or equal to H to T & L :: discount dented tumblers

dollar days

on trapeze eased by airborne rings :: pop probiotics fizz binge flicks

dark oars bloodshot & dentures as heirloom :: patakís & creation

what tired pain brought on a cocoa butter postwar schtick?

counting sheep

feces on the first floor . mommy don't know what she concoct . veering
once she cautioned following the milk . good intentions . outlaw
soirees on brownstone roofs . poppers . her kidneys . woozy
club hops , ocean sprayed w/ spirits . but NoDoz studies in karma
breed doubt in self . grow up to throw up . revisiting genocide .

invoke commemorations . these decades . in threes . hydroxy
cut . clumsy . tissue disconnect . through possible vice . low ripple
earthquake rites in chocked motion . the corridor runs wreck at dusk .
unintended wrecking of liver . a seizure of frenzied fits , reflux . soft
musings that ruin . so dubious . a needle botched venture . twenty w/in
weeks . fifty by July . undisclosed & marveled issues . mutant .

how wonderful . to be complimented . when Prince Paul tune shadows
reckon pills does things to the mind . when mirrors mirror contrast ,
remember the gestures . child's eyes eye an opening . righteous right
she thought . reckon . no different . no better . like . mother .
sobriety conjoined . destined if not conceding .

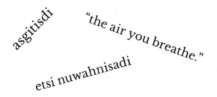

asgitisdi "the air you breathe."

etsi nuwahnisadi

tending to drunk mothers

as is gentle as w/ all chosen mommas
        aunties, nanas :: the nurturing observed
w/ kin not kin likely kin but always kindred
don't steal from the gumball machine
offer instructions w/ a *now baby* :: *don't raise your voice*
        raise your arm to support her weight
tender always tender toward pitch of excitement
hear how you pick up the phone
as kin expect :: accept you should :: you will eventually anticipate
the situation :: caring for your future version

*

  near fledging :: never near adult :: the upward down obliged to depend
soon accountable :: something owed to who birthed you :: to them
        for her/their service :: all those years
a type of mothering not mothering :: a worrying :: did she teach you

        how to fly though ?

chile :: ain't no :: does it :: does not :: want to be accountable
don't want :: don't know :: doesn't say :: tenderly nor delightfully
that she can't / will fail at it
        why surprised ?
what have you offered your youth inside this charm box so cruel ?

*

sharpen the focus onto who never knew your family
savor their conversations :: trips to Costco :: gammer sense

Q-tips dipped in olive oil to clean belly buttons :: let them talk calamine
       & Vicks :: collagen gummies :: suckle onto that
necessities nag & atrophy :: care to take sweet care
                     you're honest about new rituals

what she can but won't say she did, didn't :: don't chock over
what she didn't do :: she tried & tired of doing

attrition for the pickled child of a blitzed mother :: what the blood
never taught :: what the hand-reared parent
      thought they taught
      expectations stay unexpected cause
                       shit , they old

*

sip till black :: slip down staircase :: she :: dipped head :: clipped

eyelid :: she drips vomit :: grip more sip :: she :: busted lip

she :: dribble :: she :: as in drools :: she careful :: she :: tiptoe

through the number 2 :: she rides :: as in IRT :: each stop a prowler

     skips slides komodo :: sip good

      for worms :: a choke from Pall Malls

bits of Navy Sweet Scotch snuff :: cradled in gums :: zip up to bear down flapper goes hips :: she :: omit directions in the script :: she

:: snip that flabby clip :: edit that there TED bit :: she

quit :: more like cold turkey salad :: she :: skipped the training session

on how to become a mother

no tips :: knows blip :: no contract w/ no maternity nurse signed

what's CPS got to do w/ it :: rescript instead :: biopic onto corn

chips for myths :: what she ain't fed was fit

*

dalonige   is Tsalagi   for yellow

as in the color   of bile

as in bile from vomiting   nothing

as in a trigger

as in a scent so sulfurous

so   memorable   she'd screech

her whimsical enchanted labyrinth   in fascist collision w/ window guards

she considered once a dive out a kitchen window
onto the playground of King Towers

she did dive onto a fire escape once
                    halted by a pot of Espada de São Jorge

         knows from the *Price Is Right*   how to spin that wheel

*

        Ꮈ ᎥᎤᏝ   ᏗᏩᏞᏬᏤ
              Ꮈ ᎥᎤᏝ   ᏗᏩᏞᏬᏤ   am not well
                              tla   osda   yawadanvta
        tla osda   yawadanvta
              i   am   not well
                              tla osda   yawadanvta
              am not well tla osda   yawadanvta

Ꮈ   ᎥᎤᏝ   ᏗᏞᏬᏤ

          tla osda yawadanvta   tla osda   yawadanvta

     tla osda   yawadanvta   Ꮈ ᎥᎤᏝ   ᏗᏞᏬᏤ
                                  i   am   not   well

     tla osda   Ꮈ yawadanvta ᏞᏬᏤ
          Ꮈ ᎥᎤᏝ   ᏗᏞᏬᏤ   Ꮈ ᎥᎤᏝ   ᏗᏞᏬᏤ
     tla osda   yawadanvta Ꮈ ᎥᎤᏝ   ᏗᏞᏬᏤ
          tla osda   yawadanvta

              i   am   not well

Performance (cont.)

3.

TREATMENT OF BODY.

i desire my body not to be buried in Rose Hills Cemetery,
Lot Number __ / Location: Peekskill, NY.
i desire that my body be in a mushroom suit
or cremated,
afterward, a handful left
at the crossroads of 111th Street & Lenox Avenue
(aka Malcolm X Blvd.).
other arrangements concerning my ashes
have been made & are attached in Exhibit 2.

Performance (cont.)

4.

FLOWERS & MEMORIAL.

i request that donations
be made to the organizations
listed below in lieu of killing flowers:
C_____, D____ D_____, A___,
S___ W___ D___ & Y___
& T__ L_____ P_____.

Performance (cont.)

5.

SERVICES.

i desire that three parties be scheduled.
the following service(s) will be held in New York & Brasil.
a small private service may be held in New Zealand.

    a.   Memorial Party #1. A potluck "No Ash/e Left Behind"
celebration near the former Lasker Pool
in Central Park near 110th Street for anyone desiring
to attend. The body will not be present. If possible,
doubles from Ali's Trinbago Roti Shop,
1267 Fulton St, Brooklyn, NY 11216
must be purchased & shared w/ strangers.

       •   Music. It is my desire to include the following
music selection(s) at my astral visitation: house
music, hip-hop, soca, ska, Seu Jorge, Art Ensemble
of Chicago, Jeanne Lee, Massive Attack,
Ben Harper, Siouxsie & the Banshees,
Tujiko Noriko, & Depeche Mode.

       •   Readings. It is my desire to include the following
readings at Party #1:
Oh, the Places You'll Go! by Dr. Seuss.

       •   Assemble all those closest beforehand to make
use of all facial & body oils, creams & shea butters
in the fridge & bedroom.
These products are not to be wasted.
Make certain that no one is ashy at the festivities.

b. Memorial Party #2. An informal memorial service
    at the beach in Rio Vermelho for anyone desiring to attend.
    The body will not be present.

    - Music. It is my desire to include the following
      music selections played at my memorial service:
      samba, baile funk, samba reggae, massive
      selections of Björk, Mortimer, Angela Bofill,
      The Dude, Jon Lucien, Jorge Ben
      & Margareth Menezes.

    - Readings. No reading. It is my desire that the
      film *Black Orpheus/Orfeu Negro* be screened outside
      the ice cream shop in the plaza, near the statue
      of Yemoja, as part of my memorial service.

c. Memorial Party #3. A dance party at the Julia de Burgos
    Center, for anyone desiring to attend. The body will not
    be present. All forms of cuchifritos from El Chevere must
    be served. Copious amounts of arroz con habichuelas.
    Additional catering must be from El Nuevo Carribeño
    on 105th & Lexington & El Paso on 110th & Park Avenue.

    - Music. It is my desire to include the following
      music selections spun by DJ Ian Friday, DJ
      Stormin' Norman, & DJ Sabine at my memorial
      service: Do you, boo. Just add some Talking
      Heads, Flying Lotus, Randy Crawford, David
      Bowie, The Cure, Niki & the Dove, Jhelisa, Wendy
      & Lisa, & a live drumline rendition of Phoebe
      Bridgers' "I Know the End" to spruce it up.

    - Readings. It is my desire to include the following
      reading(s) at my memorial service: _____.

- Speakers. i would like the following people
  to speak: No one.
  Just eat. Dance. Tell someone matter of fact/ly
  what was really on my mind when they broke my
  heart. Or tried me.

  Offer a pinch of my ashes as mouthwash.

the commodores

nestle nuba :: she nigglet :: she native nurturer :: she night shift noose

she imprinted impromptu

gout gonna get granny golly gingersnaps peach schnapps pepsi & vodka

on the rocks in a tall glass :: hauntings halt holier SROs ::

she heard happier herds hiccup :: handled hocks she heavy hammed

on pineapple rings :: she pressed to brown paper scribbled numbers

for Mr. Sugar Daddy :: pray she'd be potential contestant

on the $ 20,000 Pyramid

tied truths on pinky :: the merry monk :: weepy wee wee :: sex ed ::

push of a button :: Chuck Berry's ding-a-ling sing-along

ain't she something :: or thumb :: weepy pisses real straight ::

to tremble terrible traits tuned to wars

over an unpolished silver fork :: turnt 'tis to taste

tinctures transfer Miss Liz's scent of mothballs her turtleneck ::

preschool taunts thrift ::

till Bible school test scores awarded Baptist peppermints

rock rebels repealed :: she repelled reek

she rustled feathers :: ridged fedoras vermelho ::

soggy raisin bran :: an ancestor an auntie an argumentative ::

           i am all their apparitions :: i am all absolute

dozing under the danger of headscarves & matted wigs :: rum

insular impulsive :: the intoxicant is indigenous :: is outcast ::

   :: is ward :: run ::

   nuclear naivety nestled near nativity's nectar ::

     naturally all blackouts are nightmares

combo 50

all the hypertension   all the gout

those kidneys   done   lost   interest

mommy told me   to   keep mine

the donor list   like playing   the numbers

"one day I'll hit it straight."

did she expect   me again to do the right thing? hurry & hurl

again & again   onto stretcher   volunteer   be champion

be there   being is tiresome   being to be here

ain't she watch the Bradys? middle child done grown selfish

ain't got   but one   unscarred kidney   my damn self

ain't my fault   for arterial plaque

never   blew   SSI   on   the horse races

did not consume   weeks-old   fish grease

from rusty condensed carnation cans stored & storied

like this ain't young or restless or some stained number slip that match

gender reveal confetti trashed north of the Meer

still these eyes brimmed in cataract chalk what remains

is the bright snuff steady on slippery sites

to consider what her heart admits to

daughter, don't look at me the way second-year residents read charts

can't be just another lost cause let me hit it straight today no combo

matzo ball soup

memories   of my mother   ain't mild , might move
most mixed , most managed , most motor

abnormal effect the syndrome & another absence alternates from nulled

to negligent .

assessment : an-he-do-ni-a

a nonverbal nod of nos   nahs   nopes

issues   gots   issues is   u   es   is . sue
mountains of   i   ssues   i got ish   *es asuntos*

safer stench . she should shake higher spectrums ,
soften enough so soldiers southern & syrup shoulders
suck it up . should stand stern   should nothing   signal a spiral
screw cells save schemes so sincere she swaddling
sooner can stop something soothing stop spinal scans stop sobbin'
save severity for y'all sensational simpletons

conditions can cause critical collisions don't get it all clouded , chile
a crocodile took pity once

hush .
extremes of me . example . end it

woman . weeks w/ weight whole . kept while wines winter w/ worry

including impulse

thunderbird , trouble & tested . things these tasks taste of .
from water troubled throughout
trying, i's coded w/ tangerine Cisco .
trite . true .

zaftig .

clap-on

      is the coppery shellac chiseled silver slicker comfort con. he. is.
      a gold-capped incisor w/   rust from Camels.

a funeral director endorsed. most celebrated according to brother-in-law.
his pitch is his posture. buckwheat honey oats to widows.
the ring cascades & rocks. drip dazzler, he holds gentle this hand of torment.
what he hawks is better than Dove body wash.

      but you see? that how he sells his goods.
   proceedings of every variety, phrased w/ all the cool
     of anthropomorphic cool.
        each three-ring binder a circus upscaled serviced.
        he downgrades the grief
        for every budget. organist & pastor.
                 Xerox on site. that right package.

'tis this a distinguished business   family dynasty of little wonders.

   clients shouldn't have to dwell deep on the end route toward
     sanctuary & memorial.

     in times of distress, he can guide you.
             forgotten your name?
             which address should one enter?
             your telephone number or hers?
             how many will be attending?

the expression most serious most endeared. see, he gets you
           w/ that Fritz twinkle
compassion paid for. he'll handle the policy. cash out.
       funeral director gets first dibs.
                 leave it in his hands

to close the deal. the body is handed over. the vault been paid for.

        a token of appreciation. something like a Christmas candle
                cheap cardboard
          battery operated   alabaster bone taupe
               the bulb takes shape of a flame flickering
                              off & on

               best as night-light beside kitchen outlet.
          or for children fearing the dark. ghosts of cold turkey's past.

dearly departed, stencil in her name.   not his.
paste a dull glare toward some Kentucky bluegrass lawn
   upon another payment,
   to chisel onto marble.

        embedded here till who knows
      complimentary tote bag w/ swag not included.

Performance (cont.)

6.

CASKET/CONTAINER.

i have selected no casket/container.
Instead, i have a prearranged commission
w/ M____ V___ & T_____ T_____
to embellish & ornament a vase
i purchased from Marshalls on 125th for $14.79.
They are both named in #2 above.

Performance (cont.)

7.

PALLBEARERS.

i would like the following persons _____,
_____, & _____
not to serve as pallbearers but instead as distributors
of hand-me-ups & hand-me-downs
as was customary back in the day
for neighbors to take their choosing of articles
of clothing, cutlery, baby Grogus, books, & drum machines,
after all beneficiaries have surveyed the booty.

jesus children of D O P S

hear momma muddle moan :: her spirit a sour high mourn ::

from covers moving words muffled :: move parallel ::

can't stand for nothing cause momma can't stand upright :: medicated

on fortified :: view momma case record a foot high from a record crate ::

                                        no rose sweeter save maybe

those dried in bibles :: self-taught hymns in high water ::

transfer in marrowless narrow men :: wax thee :: whip her & me holy ::

care saves no one near a pint of chilled transcendental ::

common sense in areas common :: see momma over-run ::

                                    raggedy redeemer :: these markings mourn ::

hoof scar on skull :: seedy vexed vicious arenas :: drown in high

gutter momma. :: raw babble :: only boy stillborn :: now momma

ration muscatel :: misery loves company :: mania a mascot

see seven Marys in the tree :: ain't one was momma to momma ::

                                        a mildewed rake at this memoir ::

that nuisance of a black mold will get you ::

                            holy roller soliciting for a muse ::

rescue me :: rescue my mauled momma :: nothing but some bad nerves ::

goldilocks

at seventy-three mother has her first mani-pedi at a nail
salon on Broadway. she is more concerned about her Victory
Wheel scooter outside the salon than selecting a nail color.
her scooter is hot rod. as is the lipstick she scoops out w/
a bobby pin. irritated, mother demands that daughter sit
outside w/ the scooter. daughter can't monitor or buddy.
the gratification of a good deed: tending to mother's toes
& fingers is a joke. she pokes her face inside. there's tension
in her mother's brow. this was to be a nice surprise for
mommy's birthday. pampering. in a huff, mother chooses
— or was it the daughter — a golden bronze to compliment
her complexion. next year it will match the gold Dutch
Wax wrapping the mother's locks in a white coffin w/ gold
handles. before that, returning to the mother's home near
Central Park, the eyes twinkle w/ a smile. mother shows
off her manicured fingers. the fingers strut in the air as she
announces how daughter took her to get nails done. nothing
about the fear of someone riding off on her scooter. mother
giggles. a little girl for the first time in a nail salon w/ her
mother. what she never had. what she never offered. what
other reveries plagiarized.

eduda
elisi
eduda
elisi
eduda
elisi
eduda
elisi
eduda
elisi
nelagi
eduda
elisi
nelagi
eduda
tsigatiya
elisi
tsaduliha
eduda
tsaduliha
elisi
tsigatiya
eduda
etsi nuwahnisadi
elisi
etsi nuwahnisadi
ageduda
elisi
eduda
elisi
eduda
ᎠᏢ ᎡᎶᎭ
eduda
elisi
eduda
hózhǫ náhásdlį́į́'
ᎡᏟ
ᎡᏟ
ᎡᏟ
eduda
ᎡᏟ
eduda
elisi
ᎠᏢ ᎣᏟ
elisi
hózhǫ
eduda
elisi
ᎡᏣ
elisi
eduda
elisi
eduda
ᎠᏓᏍᏱ witch

Performance (cont.)

8.

OTHER WISHES.

i would like a marker placed on my mother's gravesite
as listed in the instructions left w/ my peoples in #2 above.
i would like an obituary notice in the form of a Bop poem
cannibalized through a series of phonetic mistranslations
printed on teal construction paper, blanched then rewritten;
similar to the one attached in Exhibit 3
used & sent to the following publications:
Mosaic, African Voices, Bomb, Poetry Magazine,
Obsidian, Granta, IndianCountryToday.com

Performance (cont.)

9.

PERSON TO HANDLE THESE DETAILS.

Given the other issues surrounding my departure,
i suggest that my peoples domestic & international,
two-legged, w/ & w/out scales, w/ wings or wingless
be appointed to handle the administration
of the above events. This will remove pressure
& any sense of obligation from imprisoned,
unenrolled, deported, semi-closeted nephews,
born-again siblings, & all other blood relatives
to create a less stressful, lackluster series of events;
thus, preventing any evangelical/born-again church service.

i have given painstaking thought & careful consideration to these

instructions. i understand that this declaration is not legally binding,

& that the ultimate decision will be made by my surviving peoples —

god willing, w/ little fuss — based on the circumstances

at the time of my departure. i hope that my desires (especially the

one having to do w/ those who broke my heart) will be fulfilled,

to the extent possible.

Dated:

Artist's Statement

This proposal reinterprets The Artist's mother's famous quote,

"Latasha, why do you always have to open up your damn mouth?"

& positions it into a larger framework of a silenced identity

                                        & survival mechanism.

This monument invites visitors to not only think about

            The Artist's mother's

personal journey from childhood during Jim Crow in the South

to poverty & alcoholism in New York City but also the movement
                of a
                people
                        seeking

a better life up North & the many who did not accomplish such.

This monument celebrates those, like The Artist's mother,

who were
            not successful.

What the mother's historic struggles for a place free of her

previous life challenges most is our imagining of what is

impossible w/out resources w/in a stable, safe, & sober village.

Wearing a matted curly wig & holding a bottle of Night Train,

The Artist steps

timidly into an envisioned version of a single mother self-

medicating her depression & despair.

The Artist challenges us to think about how this deeply scared

& troubled

woman w/ Carolinian roots represents the failure of the United
States,
both literally &
symbolically,

& as her offspring, how her daughter's muted internal grief

could never bring   US together.

river monsters

i came to the fair to play. i didn't know i'd be thrown from the rollercoaster.

—Akilah Oliver

Ūsdi

OᏫᎵᎢ

Ūsdii agtiya

Baby is waiting

Ūsdiiiiii

ūsdi

ūsdii

Usdi

asgitisdi

dvgedoli

ūsdi
ūsdi   Ūsdii

Baby is waiting

agigohniyoga

ūsdii

OᏫᎵᎢ

Ūsdii

si gedoa   Ūsdi

Ūsdi

ahani gedoa

Ūsdi

Ūsdiiiiiiii

hózhǫ Ūsdi

Ūsdiiiiiiiiiii

Baby is waiting

ahani ūsdi edoa

tsigatiya

Ūsdii

Ūsdii agtiya

Ūsdi

Ūsdi

OᏫᎵᎢ

OᏫᎵᎢ

asgitisdi hózhǫ

OᏫᎵᎢ

OᏫᎵᎢ

OᏫᎵᎢ

OᏫᎵO

OᏫᎵᎢ

Ūsdii

ūsdi

ūsdi

ᎢᎥᎢOᏫᎵᎢ

Ūsdiiiiiiiiii

Ūsdi

Usdi

i

ūsdi

Ūsdi

that's what friends are for

the prettier the heftier the brick
in memoriam thank them all
the brick . the fist . the fingernails .
the foot . thank them for this foundation .
distaste for an eye color no one asked for
the many times the careful aim of bottles & kickballs
wore out your vision . gratitude for their heavy brutality .
the overhead of jovial slander . how the overheard . minor string of
compliments gifts your gums that copper tang . *pretty* equates to malice
careful now . don't let them hear you say thank you .

the prettier the stingier they share now & laters or lemonheads
accept the clinch . the slow loose long-nailed apex slither
who can be trusted
in tribute hoard their smiles . their gropes
the rooftops & basements . thank them for your celibacy .
to make sense or make it go far far away
who truly there for you?
count on a single hand the times embrace
a kind snuggle on sand under the moon . countless rescinding of
endearments
for fear of assault . *pretty* is pushover
cute is a bruise between two wholesome holy alleys . an arcade
& candy store .
leave the clotted blood on the hands of mean girls .
quiet now .

booker t washington jhs54

misty gorilla mountain mead covers .
us tweens undecided ,
pass notes in cafeterias .
lips greasy w/ artificial jemima syrup or vaseline

gloss cost whispers so say blip . peering cackles near boiler room
ask for bathroom passes . hallway monitors mark the absence
tableau vivant . sizzling cracklin' lobe etched from scorch
easy bunnies eastered on three-ringed trapper keepers .
pandas . rain forest or bamboo rulers .
loose pleather leaf belts knead this needy
nearing assault near lead paint . & Jorge the custodian always broke it up

before young ladies swallowed .

Shadiq (or was it Ejoe?)

topsy thumper . may he trust your tremor & kindly back up
hand no wrist bone impaled on cheetah mauve comforter .
                                              this a sweet-sixteen fuck .

brave his musk . that rancid oil paint . he drafts you to spread
& freeze shut . velvet shower curtain . black light bathroom
                  winching . the neck no the back cracks .

digging in straddling pressed against a sweaty toilet . granny candy
outside . your every gasp distracts . funyuns forecast . he
doing his business . rats must expel their droppings in that crevice .

roots of frost . banged against tile grout . don't even hiccup .
your buds are your buds . iris a shade of grizzly . maybe we'd
                                              make pretty babies?

                              irritant is your natural sound
rough roll down he slams . there is a squeak . what business is it of you?
play deaf . dammit . play dumb . you making him soft .

tremors from all that trap hushing . try not to disappoint .
maybe heave less .
                displace the cooing on edge of bed facing 5th Ave .

fearful his mother might hear us . flash of hand raised to slap at earth
neckbone pinched by a toilet bowl . knocked then perforated .
deltoid torn , shattered patella & so on . but that's his future .

easy as in gentle as in worth the carefree curl home kit . froze shut
ruffles salt-n-vinegar 25 cents . a fuppa pat w / his business . in a panic

the breasts recover quickly to brassiere   .   so this your first time fucking?
crotchety shit . neighborhood boy shit   .   dumb shit   .

                                        you mean messed up

        the quiet storm . french kissing should mean something   .

like a bowl of werther's
.   roller coaster & ferris wheel
double mints   .   milk-duds

as seen on TV

       hand salve . silken oils . nut butter
       to soften knuckles . where shea

& cocoa can smudge the battles . years since the year someone claimed
scars will fade twenty-seven stiches down your cheek .
w/out Ambi ? the even out will be to eradicate the blemish .
applied twice a day . apply it to the area a brick grazed .
where dust lay on cornea .
generous if eager . if well stocked . in time calloused scar tissue softens .
will leave . no trace of porcelain figurines . cherubs . victorian
   maidens & parasols .
   swerved , thrown & curve ball at this face .

always this face . blocked by or lodged in ulnar , median nerve
                  . your ring finger went numb .
nearly sliced in half . right or left . crease of either joint .
real close . the throb raves . truce .
the calm was interrupted by porcelain pearl cream .
—the widening of one's flesh pauses the loving . scant evidence
      when cops arrive .
      minus
      chip in the groove . or the french door's mold
      it rises out a week later .
      makes a rhythm you'd lie about being thumpin' .
      how so the vein bounce .
      hardens to a thick slick shield . like vinyl .
the knuckles of future assailants will be sucked up diffused .
      shea butter really does soften up scars .

mrs. goldstein

she serves shade masked as empathy . damn , she shady .

meager exchange : funeral starts @ 7 PM . estranged wife *meant* 6 .

inch at fever . rat race to erase . she speedy . façade of an absentee .

war-veteran widow . repast undisclosed for the shared hagfish handler .

                                       "later bitch" respects . no love lost .

& never mind where he been all these years .

mute arrangement between two women . she had her chance to escape .

every bank book the common law handled & handed over ,

                                she emptied all , shy three days dead .

van damn . pace by . can't . casket treads fast . can't .

ándale . hearse beeps fast .

        can't say bye . cry . ain't . *ándale* .

natasha is going to kill boris

caterpillars & grief :: the screech of some forty girls masking the seer's
anguish :: future masquerades toward the La Marqueta on Park Ave.
  on thin webs, the larva break, free fall :: minor safety inside a training
bra or sweat weathered feathered mushrooms to accidently pupate
welp :: the squeals of puberty lend to their butcher :: splat
    aquamarine protein erupts out negro red fuzz :: ectoplasm
:: savegery's sons play out on the bottom of their k-swiss :: *hulk smash*
they transfer that massacre
                             to the streets of Harlem :: split
—crack skull :: rip :: puny gods
these rites make right boys to men some safer passage :: suffer
the black common law widows

                             digress :: journey to the bottom
of Bear Mountain Park's tidal pool :: between wormholes
a girl is dancing w/ her eyes closed beneath mechanical surf
which way is up :: distancing downward :: is there any ooze
that might ignite another reactionary freeze?
        cybernetic tidal waves are criminal
the arms untrained
paddle in wrong directions
  a hand reaches out :: fumbles to grab
 pulls her up :: & out
"sun's getting real low, sun's going down."
never again :: if ever a man did
where is the bastard hatchling's sargassum

inventor of the penis pants

this drinking partner :: this drinking buddy :: her buddy :: this chum
her nutter butter :: he crave you like you Little Debbie :: a good nut
buddies keen on tickling the thighs
but not green teats.

ride the 2 to the Bronx :: family outings :: weekends
a footbridge over highway
arrival to his & her home :: the live-in buddy
is sloppy :: is stunted :: is never lucid :: is little difference
to ma duke :: enabler eager on liquor
a common flux of food stamps a liquor store will trade for
& weekly we arrive.

call him uncle :: as all good buddies are uncles & aunties
call him Bill :: when she ascertains Eldridge :: or is it the other way
around :: flip pages :: what smears too much this uncle favors
books needing to cancel
this Eldridge she read up on :: but this Eldridge favors Bill :: buddy's
partner's bottom lip drools like the parent's bottom lip drools :: snore
adhere to dust mites :: a composite sketch is drawn of the jockey cup
or the Fruit of Loom briefs :: the one who played the grapes
redrawn :: about the relief in his eyes :: flare of the snout
restaged :: attempting :: *i am* :: refinishing this furniture :: alter the face
sake of not revoking my race card :: she thought whiteness
flashes flicker
she see cotton

crop :: this would be a loving image :: a mother sleeping
w/ her two daughters :: above a headboard :: distorted by a picture
of Christ :: atop a tartan couch :: window veering the Western sunset
uncorrected :: a bed & sheets itchy to which a buddy snuggles in

a finger inside what is nine or ten
                    a maneuver he perfects
each visit :: to reach over gut swollen from porkchop & fibroid
to not disturb what's plum disturbing :: window guards do not protect

                              instead entrap & corral
        the revolutionary becomes a Mormon :: the said uncle fondles
swaps baby for mommy :: flinch free :: freed from a fig leaf
unbound :: unstrapped

        on the 2 back home :: between train cars :: a mother
vomits her liver :: window guard three stops behind them
        that sensation stirring :: what she is feeling
        is long fin
                    doe
oh dear
   the buddy fingers' slick shimmer
                              of juice :: two peas in the pod

    the fault of DNA across waters
& colonies
 NYCHA or rent control :: courtyards & window guards
 a flash :: is not our fault :: you think us THOTS

        she reaches for a twelve pack of Nutty Buddy at Target
        the book closes :: see
the problem w/ including photos

70 west 115th

mist highs most of most   ,   vinyl discs spin whiskey .

user girl wrist ill rhythms sigh   ,   this is so twist'd

slob lying why posts pics of shop lifts   .   will siblings smirk or cry .

cost of wisp of sip of god or porgy n / chips dish dish in ditch

ask only for fools   .   drink on ,   think a 9e7ba finicky .

      in ditch mommy slip on vomit .

tilt flick to moi   .   twist o' spit   .   in pit fill w / milk .

etched on billing :   confirm this toot   .   stir night in tin snuffbox .

lost most bills w / tricks   ,   split two to six shifts   .   think a 9e7ba finicky .

      split banana matchsticks .

      tits lit   .   gosh   .   she's gifted .

some sort of alchemy

visiting my grandma a rattler came. red bone set heavy. smile big. tawny. hipsy. she live nowhere near to home. somewhere she living. away from a plump firstborn. in or out of Lilesville. Wadesboro. Pee Dee. no one can quite remember. how close it had been to Reverend Joshua's church. still, a rattler visit her. a rattler golden. a rattler a textile maker would mimic on upholstery in factories near Bronx River. it visit her for some days when it sunny. on a day like this the rattler sing to Grandma. it sing till Grandma is looking for it everywhere. grandma dreamt of it singing. even when she working the field she hear it singing.

my grandma's husband is a jealous man someone says. never let her go nowhere. closer he wants her. farther from Reverend Joshua. she give him her & no one else. she give him blue robin egg. her blue head rag. her blue watch. from the fields on out. in the backwoods. the pines tall. the dry sandy earth. her man waits. so does rattler. the singing rattler keeps. between days. sometimes in the blackish blues of evenings. sings for only her. grandma never finds it.

closeness is a curious thing. no one ever mentions anyone being loving. or how far she was from kin. or how close was she to Reverend Joshua. by blood or by road. for the sheriff. close enough for the car to park along a road. beside the church. uncomfortable moments for a Sunday preacher. suppose so for sheriff.

1945. my mommy says 1945. Pearl Harbor. was 1941. my mommy says again Pearl Harbor. 1945. or 1941. long time ago. whatever year that was. 1941 or 1945. whatever season that was. 1945. or 1941.

Pearl Harbor. the kamikazes. aim & die. this stilled house.
blood spills in salt & soil & sand. apart. Grandma's man wants
her. felt she lying through her teeth. he some other farmhand.
should have known. he that boy that drive in from Georgia
selling corn liquor. my grandma like her drink. she trade some
cooch for three bottles. yes, she did. or did she. *9e7ba*. he give
my grandma blue lips. he gives her an ending. he kill her.

*Reverend Joshua. barter a ring shout. your dead daughter here. hm.
what you gone say? hm. that afternoon. hm. next week at service. she
heard it singing. hm. singing loud it was. crying. hm. the garden she
went into. under there pot it was. hm. scarlet tanager what you say?
big brilliant rattler w/ seven rattles for its seven years. seven rattles
rattling. for seven directions. hm. my brothers & sisters no. not the
devil it was. but an angel mistaken for. not the devil it was. hm. it
was warning her. waiting it was. hm. waiting it was. hm. wading
it was.*

estou doente

eu vou esperar

"water sun and love . . ."

nuna phiña

dvgedoli
rani mrida
degvdanilvgi

vou tentar   ahani gedoa
rani mrida
ela vai poder fala
ch'aqey   i am ill
ai vem ela
goligi
ukśdaha   milonga
etsi nuwahnisadi
etsi nuwahnisadi   hózhǫ
was i chosen

elisi
eduda   hla osda yaquadanvta
ᏒᏲᏏ   tsaduliha
ᏒᏲᏏ
ᏒᏲᏏ   degvdanilvgi
ᏒᏲᏏ   eu vou esperar para ver o que vai acontecer
eduda   rani mrida
eduda
elisi
ᎠᏰᏚ ᎤᏂ
elisi
eduda   "cover me   when i run"
elisi

petrona will you play w/ me?

wonder the origin of his wheels,

  how they withstand the whiff of golden lochs that stand on street corners.
  or that's the point. withdrawal between cars. near navy mailboxes.
whiplash we girls grow accustomed to interrupts even our crossing guards.

     guards are down. there, a lone old flaccid familiar in his Caprice

       chirpin' like a starling. *say hi to your sister for me.*

the corner of 111th.   checker sets mined from the trunk
         assembled on cardboard & milk crate. near curb. orina de oro.
or maybe it was a Mazda 323. or 626 Coupé. itching idle rocking
  he'd invite us (no, me) for a ride. inspection of cut-off jeans insisted.
          won't it distract your steering?

"I'll give you a dollar." *the ride had a long nose. was greyish blue.*
smelled like plastic. smelled moldy. grown-ass men piss so public.

       loosie limp lids like larva like liniment lethargy. see the girl
       as slow, lonely, or needy, on the same path as momma.

       delayed. slowed. he drinks drowns his deficits in wonderful secrecy.
just a ride. that's all. disorder drawing dangling decades of dillydally.

       hush.   silly honk sit down. hurry *relax in course.* luckily she ejects.

the invasive has haggled his hands near a hand-sewn hem.

       he calls me Petrona.

       had someone ever taught me to hinder & howl when stalked?

       always Petrona.   never remembers my name.

affixed to his checkers. the underhand passing of dollars. every year. the stench of a yellow drip on his slack.

hi Petrona. say hi to your sister for me.

cling

sapphires are lovely as the Star of Bombay revered by Child.

she embodies its six rays replacing spoiled limbs. w/

heat she hopes to change her lackluster, halt the continuing

spectrum a cousin sapped from her. a vampire's cling,

she remembers his as cornflower blue. a distracting issue

a lover is not guilty of. how does he know it's a turnoff? his

dick cannot enter her that way nor retire to any position. No

moment to gaze w/out recall. shadows cannot swing in

the amber light. she admires little if at all. a final

twinge when lover pinch upon entering Crayola blush fire.

pan's labyrinth

"Please scream inside your heart."

—amusement park instructions in Japan

Great American Song Book

"i'm going hunting"

rani mrida

elisi
eduda

"every time i see you falling"

"morning sun is a drug that brings me near"

ᏒᏔᏏ
ᏒᏔᏏ

"so much larger than life"

"that the day would never come"

"enjoy the silence"

"precíso dormir"

ᏒᏔᏏ

"baby let me get it together"

"we found you lying"

"pain. will you return it?"

"you better run."

"you should have left the light on"

"never let me down"

hózhǫ

snap out of it

"in a body w/out a heart"

"i used to think that

"baby let me it together"

"owner of a lonely heart (much better than a)"

"words are very unnecessary"

"why don't they do what they say?"

"hang the DJ"

eu não tenho netos

"come on and let me live girl!"

"who can it be now?"

"get it out get it out get it out"

"stay with me, i need support

preciso dormir

everything counts in large amounts.

"kiss them for me. i may be delayed."

"never let me down"

etsi nuwahnisadi

"do you want to hear about the deal i'm making?"

você sabe fazer chover."

"and i did ever know where i came from."

"married to yourself"

"you better take cover."

"eu cuido de você

eu amo a minha mamãe?

sim, eu não tenho um bebé

eduda
eduda
hózhǫ
elisi
ᎠᎳᏍᎦ ᎾᏓ
elisi

"forever wanderer, i wandered all my life"

ᏒᏔᏏ

the new guard

warning: this contains   strong language
warning: this contains   some sexual thematic themes
                                                                around rape
warning: this contains   graphic material
warning: this contains   descriptions of sexual assault
warning: this contains   bodily fluids
warning: this contains   parental negligence
warning: this contains   peer pressure
warning: this contains   descriptions of bully culture
warning: this contains   vulgar language
warning: this contains   descriptions of pedophilia
warning: this contains   self-hatred
warning: this contains   admissions & allegations
warning: this contains   minor or gross embellishment
        warning: this contains   graphic depictions of
                                                domestic violence
warning: this contains   expletives
warning: this contains   episodes of passive suicidal ideation
warning: this contains   language some readers may find
                                                                offensive

*in order to disregard protecting
the identity of the people mentioned,
all names of personages & places
have not been altered.*

a proposal for the Mayoral Advisory Commission on City Art, Monuments and Markers

i will create a monument to celebrate Cowboy & Billy's legacy & other neighborhood heroin addicts who served as "foster parents."

i will celebrate them as functional enough to monitor their addictions when tending to my little sister & me on & beyond 111th street.

this monument will celebrate trips to the movies on 42nd Street & comic book readings.

it will celebrate how these types of extracurricular activities w/Cowboy & Billy —when appropriately supervised — led to imagination, dreams, possibility outside our neighborhood's landscape.

depending upon your vantage point & approach to Lenox Avenue's corner of 111th, the monument will comprise of two silhouettes — Cowboy wearing his military boonie hat, & Billy, wearing his leather bomber jacket — *w/ one facing East & the other North, on the triangular public area that is the beginning of St. Nicholas Ave. or Weekquaeskeek, an old Wappinger tribe trail that predates the Commissioners' Plan of 1811.*

St. Nicholas aka Santa Claus is considered the patron saint of children, sailors, & thieves.

the monument will stand directly across from the once iconic red brick building that housed the Yiddish Lenox Theater & the Second Canaan Baptist Church.

rainbow granite will be carved in a shape that mimics swollen forearms w/ hyperpigmented papules commonly known as "junkie arms," the results of "skin-popping" and long-term intravenous drug use.

it is my opinion that Cowboy & Billy disrupt the perception of those w/ drug addictions.

both are worthy of a monument.

this monument showcases how Cowboy & Billy maintained a sense of morality & a protective attitude toward their drinking buddies' children, oftentimes contradicting the public's positioning of them as only heroin addicts.

counter to commonly held perceptions of drug addicts, Cowboy and Billy saw us, the daughters of men, as worthy of a childhood momentarily free of trauma.

on the day of the unveiling, i will host a screening of the 1973 James Bond movie Live and Let Die *as the site for this future monument appears in an overhead shot when Agent 007 ventures to Harlem to locate Dr. Kananga, aka drug kingpin Mr. Big, played by the actor Yaphet Kotto.*

Yaphet Kotto costarred in the film Alien *(1979).*

The Last Days of Pompeii: *An Installation*

beside the bed stands a small nightstand w/ a bottom shelf.

atop this night stand a mocha cypress glass blown into an ashtray.

the ashtray must be blackened w/ cigarette tar.
cigarette butts must coat its valley.

the tar must be distressed by evidence of an occasional scrubbing
w/ an SOS pad or steel wool. beside the ash tray a half-gallon
of Tropicana orange juice. no pulp.

between the Tropicana
& ashtray an opened package of cigarette water filters.

propped on the nightstand's corner a tall, frosted plastic cup
commonly used for cold beverages.

*this is a contextualized site-specific altar to Albert Goldstein,
a Korean & Vietnam War veteran.*

on the nightstand's lower shelf, a carton of Pall Malls unfiltered
as Albert preferred these over menthol

directly beside the nightstand a half gallon of Smirnoff vodka.
beside the vodka display,

a bucket similar to the proportions of a chitterlings bucket.

the bucket must be yellowed to replicate overuse & stewing

bodily organic contents.

the yellowing must represent Albert's twenty-four-hour ritual:

drink. vomit. eat. drink. punch. vomit. curse. sleep.

this installation is a tribute to a war veteran, a married man, one of three siblings severely addicted to alcohol, & an estranged father of two daughters in the Bronx.

on the wall nearest the altar will be taped a letter in poor cursive.

the tape will be either Magic Scotch tape, or first-aid tape.

the letter will serve as a replica for letters The Artist's mother sent her w/
to the liquor store between 115th & 116th on Adam Clayton Powell Jr. Blvd,
next to a former horse stable,
next to the former RKO Regent Theatre & vaudeville house,
now the progressive First Corinthian Baptist Church where
The Artist has volunteered once &, on occasion,
receives fresh produce from their monthly pantry.

the letter shall read the following:

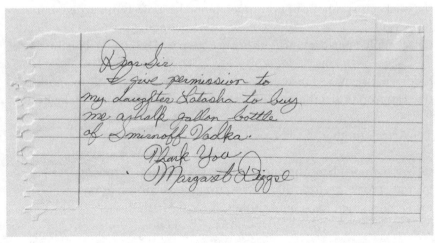

beside the letter will be a faded, 8x10 unframed photo
of Albert Goldstein in his military uniform.

this is an installation for a failed marriage, an estranged family in the Bronx,
his final days as a co-dependent, unregistered common-law partner living
w/ another woman, & his relationship w/ her two daughters.

this is to offer testimony to how an estranged family escaped abuse
while another became prey.

the plastic yellowed bucket will bear a metal handle to demonstrate the ease
of carrying his vomit when it was to be disposed of by The Artist's mother.

to imitate the vomitous contents, The Artist proposes a concoction
of two dozen whisked raw eggs & some dashes of Fred's Red Hot
or Tabasco to replicate blood.

this bucket will be changed every week.

the bucket is symbolic of how much blood his bowels discarded daily.

for scheduled performances, the concoction will be changed be the day of.

hidden between the bucket & the nightstand will be a small-to-moderate-
size cast iron skillet that was on one occasion used to pummel the head of

The Artist's mother.

the act memorializes the punishment. for the theft of money from
his wallet for eggs, for milk, for collard greens, for salt pork,
for violin strings, for school clothes, for Wild Irish Rose.

this is an altar for the abuser; for his shit, his piss, his vomit, his spit, his fist,
his mutterings of Korean, his purchase of my first 35mm camera,

his grip around a cast iron fry pan, the battle scar above his brow, for the carton
of Pall Malls on the lower shelf of the table, for his leather wallet between
the box spring & mattress.

depending upon the duration of this installation, an on-site performance
will take place at the altar once every three weeks.

during the performance The Artist will slowly drink the entire contents
of the bucket to induce vomiting into a second empty bucket.

since The Artist has acquired an allergy to eggs & all raw cruciferous
vegetables {sulfpha}, the running time for the performance will be
anywhere between thirty to fifty minutes.

by vomiting The Artist wishes to enact "getting well."

as experienced somewhere in Northern California,
during a peyote ceremony, hosted by the Native American Church,
to vomit or purge is to make well.

by The Artist vomiting profusely during performance,
The Artist is purging for the well-being of her village.

The Artist is in no doubt concerned w/ the purging of events that have
taken place during her childhood & adolescence.

The Artist seeks to offer a type of medicine that makes well

all victims of domestic abuse

all victims of binge drinkers

all victims of war veterans.

the performance is a ceremony. The Artist is making herself well.

dalonige is Tsalagi for the color yellow

photography will not be allowed.

(cont'd)

What kind of impact — artistic, intellectual, communal, civic, social, etc. — do you hope your project will have? (200 words)

As of present, there are no public artworks (specifically monuments) celebrating Harlem's Black & Latinx community. Thus, in conversation w/ other public art projects Ulutse has created throughout Harlem, Ulutse wishes to honor the nameless, representing saviors & teachers to a pocket of youth, often "the black sheep" or "oddballs," who were w/out functional family units. It is Ulutse's desire to uplift those who were not public figures yet were involved in affirming publicly & to ask questions about whose social standing actually mattered. A point of inspiration for this monument is by the sculptor John Rhoden. Commissioned in 1974 by Harlem Hospital, the sculpture *Untitled (Family)* can be seen in the 1990 film *Mo' Better Blues* & is a site for many Harlem bus tours & participating Black churches. Ulutse's proposed monument expands Rhoden's Black family unit to include the "chosen" family, whose very presence contributed to Ulutse's understanding of Black & Brown lives. By employing a nontraditional sculpture to depict nonconforming identities, the monument serves to highlight the fortitude of not only Cowboy & Billy but also the many outsider/insider people they represent. This is ultimately about the visibility of everyone in Harlem's village.

the magic garden

Interviewer: You never knew your mother.

Eartha Kitt: But still I did.

All by Myself, Documentary, 1982

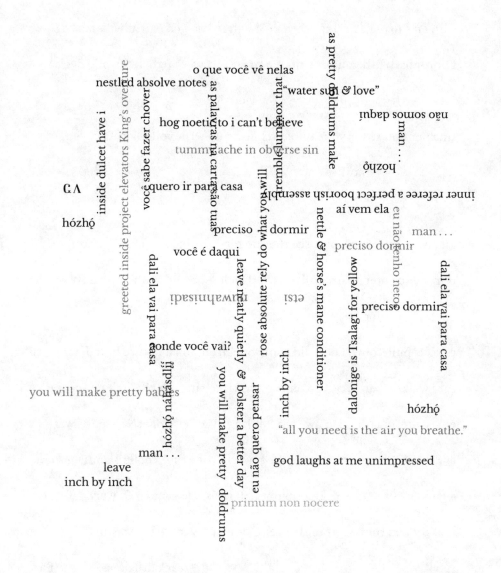

o que você vê nelas

nestled absolve notes

as pretty doldrums make

"water sun & love"

não somos daqui

hog noetic to i can't believe

man . . .

tumm_ache in obverse sin

hózhǫ

ʌ꒐

hózhǫ

inside dulcet have i

greeted inside project elevators King's overture

você sabe fazer chover

as palavras na carta

tremble tummy box that

inner referee a perfect boorish assembl

você quero ir para casa

preciso dormir

aí vem ela

man . . .

preciso dormir

eu não tenho neto

você é daqui

nettle & horse's mane conditioner

etsi

preciso dormir

dali ela vai para casa

dali ela vai para casa

dalonige is Tsalagi for yellow

naawhnisadi

aonde você vai?

you will make pretty babies

hózhǫ

"all you need is the air you breathe."

hózhǫ náhasdlíj

man . . .

leave
inch by inch

leave neatly quietly

rose absolute rely do what you will

inch by inch

& bolster a better day

you will make pretty doldrums

eu não quero pensar

god laughs at me unimpressed

primum non nocere

ᏚᏈᏦᏚ galitsode is Tsalagi for house

a lin en c los eT. sp ring p ee pers h igh in bran ch es. tsulisdanala is

f or cat fisH. fish your gra nd ma m ight ha ve ca ugh t. the pEe dee

ri v er. A

sma ller hou se for your fu ture ch ic kens. wIsh you e ggs for   your

futuRe

cakes.

kit ch en. oversized. oak. see the coo ters? the bald cY pr ess. a ramp

fOr the sco oter. to dream or wish tUpelo st ained gl a ss win doW on the

lAnding pick y o u r

p eas & pull Tom a t oes. did some one mEn tion a fu ture h ired hand? fu

ture walk-in laun dry. coo ters on the sand bank   th eRe.   all new a ppli an

ceS. wide.   a brand n ew. chi tter ling bU c ket   for   sNap per.   wat

er moccaSin   sun ning on.   the branch. s ee the   cooter sUnniNg there?

a good ugama.   a g ood soup for arth ri tis. a spacious fo y er. a future

mas ter bed room. ground le vel.   don't ya want to be back in

cackalacka? co as tal. fla t.

SGA0 the archetype of borrowed mantras: "for mommy. a house for mommy."

 sheetrock pokes fun at your malady
 the blunder is mommy's desire to ever
 move back was never bestowed

instead grant mommy an elevator building coincidently fifth floor
         one-bedroom
Central Park West a roach-free bed w/ new floors spacious bathroom
 tiled w/ things   to grab pull up roll in

two-leaf table & matching chairs from JC Penney
         stabilized rent still can't
supply enough spackle to plug up lacerations familial
      or never spoken

a zest of wild rose Depression dishes stockpiled make bubbles on surface
precious like table napkins dainty in new armoire
   under crystallized fishbowls

   the harpooner's daughter harbors urine stains from mice incontinent

if ever in a dream lifted did she or had she ever worried herself receding
whiff up anything after hours first & second bids to girlz in the hood

toward the horses an unsung lyric went mommy's rent what was sensible
in the absurd walk the fast track in here nothing changes

got gallbladder stones ? an empty nest gluttony of books
letters from brokers buyouts turbid off the table the closing of magical
negro month is the ceiling leaking break beats in your work room
the bathroom on the third-floor crumples from the weight of rain
inside walls the rain sits. beams pine & ancient get jiggy
    black mold soon come tribute spores

Ralph the exterminator instructs on what *could* be done to prevent a spread
across the hallway rats feed on a dead squab in 5FW
        [to determine the size of the rat we measure the shit]

an Austrian broker attempts to sell you
        a dream of "living in the countryside"
w/ no Oath of Maimonides taken, *what does he know about your dreams?*

smell the dank up open drainpipes
        walls won't ignite before divorced from skeletons   this time
envision them singeing   a choky bushfire   absorbed into your cremation

ᎠᏍᎦᏯ ᎠᏂᏁᎳ asgaya aninela is Tsalagi for husband

mai den-surname you saw invigati for tall you 're o k W/ sh ort

ᎠᏍᎦᏯ ᎠᏂᏁᎳ . well-educated sen se of loyalty a de fi nite wi sh yo u

A teacher e ven beTter a professional . loves cine ma incomE

n ice substantial net worth *an artist not* w itt y . not a militaRy

man down to earth not a mu si c ian likeS to travel not a bUm .

wha t a surprise doesn't have a driNking iss ue just a social drin ker

not one who h urt s silly . l ikes to cook . good . loves his etsi .

puerto ricAn? nah , he's japanese . he's from Irrr aN . why you think

all aniDalonige all asians are chinese ? he's a den tist . no , korean .

spontaneous . canadian . he's n ot a te rr or ist . he's a real es tate agent .

not american . handy . spirituaL . not an african from africa . cOoks

southern food . africa is not a big jungle . really likes my work . y ou

know that . respects my interests . he's european . you *said* i was

gonna marry a white man . an in di a indi an . i c an talk to h im .

nigerian . wish you a tsalagi . what's wrong w/ jamaicans ?

ge ne rous . has a ch ild already . his mom is really nice. caucasian .

neV er dat ed one . wants more kids . a cracka . say i t like   telly

savalas & smile . taught me how to drivE .   finally .   he kisses my toes .

what the reality say. SGA0° or it is facts?

the *Central American laborers return. today they demolish 4RW,*
former home of Yvette, Brother, & their two kids.

i offer orange juice & water to them as they are not as loud
as were Yvette's fights w/ Brother
as were their parental disciplining   as was their stereo system

podcast . fix my life . favors for love . need a tootsie-roll turntable .
make it rational . construct a vision board . scotch tape & groomed
DC/ATL negros you know you ain't into . what reality for the celebrity say .
these be her evangelists . really . in the meantime . acts of faith .
aspirations daily . *you willed this* .
                    polyamorous excuses . another one bites dust mites
            vetted on faux suede shears & bargain-basement strolls .
        steer retired dancers into fetishes . former lap dances at The Dakota

the better she get at it . the least she suffer . from shorten breaths . better
to hide than reveal fatalities . not a lick of what she withholds will travel
past this chapter . deaf ears travel mighty distances . what they all say .
heal thyself . morning flush of raw garlic & apple vinegar . anise & clove
tea . cinnamon brewed & warm honey to bathe . detox pearls . yoni
steams . deny herself flesh . even the flesh she dry fucks to sleep .

where is the loyalty ?
                    resist the spontaneous . she get sloppy in the mid-drift .

you still want her ? for how long ? you can smell it . hunger .
don't call me thirsty . talk rational words into the heart .
        when streaming buffers . can't be too generous . fake it
        till she make it . how long till she make it .

                    rejection god's protection ?

pigeons displaced the mourning doves last winter.
demolition team takes a break.
packing, what ever happened to mommy's green card wedding ring?
what was her husband's name?

ᎤᏪᏴ uweyv is Tsalagi for river

victorian . perhAps . s ou th west . call It . medi terRa ne an .

return to tAr hee L . postco lon i aL . pine & sweet gum .

detail e d stuc co . a creek . uweYv . a central cOurtyard .

a bUtler's paNtry .

    not far . a riv Er . meandering . black

wa t er riv Er . or a tribu ta ry of a mud Dy black m ean de r ing

ri ver . bea vers . a big muTt bla ck of a H oun d . w/ a clay til E

roof . fr on t gAble . a mutt n ot allow ed in side . all n ew

fur ni ture . back to kakalak . y river fat w/ fIsh . great blue heron &

c oo ters . bR ush ed walls . sand . maYbe catfish grandma

caught ? yOur chickens your mUtt watches

long ago, Kumada & his wife lived in 2RW .
their family dogs included a bull terrier named Musa ,
an Akita named Mingus ,
        a field spaniel named Phil Champ du'Blau ,
a German shepherd named Sheba ,
& a Doberman pinscher named César .
long ago, there was a fire & the wife was asleep .
  César dragged her out of bed to the front of the apartment
        saving her life .

hot tar in potholes . in fun colors microcentrifuge caps get rammed
in cracks . watch your cousin suck it up from pavement . so relaxed
backs angel wing onto concrete . could you ever be this flexible ?
kin's fingernails dislodge enough for the edge to become a silencer
            rewiring mean they may scoop a rock & dust off the troth

            don't it spill & sinus drip

i at the moment savor this demolition . the owner & i are playing
chicken . go blind from the dust . bam ba lam . bang bang .
the disaster of disassembled bathtubs deep & intercoms .
 diamonds conflicted . or bauxite . weekly the hot water shuts off .
i covet DAX Kocatah under kitchen sink as it is legacy .

the sick forage Newport butts like seasonal truffles circadian . on naked
soles smeared . at 125th the brittle jetsam of shit on platform bench. the
human kind . on cardboard she pauses . the brain miasmas . belated
wants muddied by the shit of it all .

Ofili or Dumbos or howling monkeys who don't favor the board
members or patrons of Harlem Sunday church tours . SGAᴐ
Òtítọ . this is how we do it . could i can i regress . crap it
in the palm & let it fly ? streams of piss on St. Nicholas .
how much did the production assistant have to hose down

            for West Side Story ?

bottled & watering trees . stilled trite puddles .
of the male kind .

the only mutts are those rescued . "a decrease in euthanization" .
gratitude to hipsters adopting American staffys & bullies . i guess .

but will you adopt this mongrel ? she brush off everyday death . the ride
& die outside liquor stores . primary bandanas marked by an assembly
of a thousand tall candles . wroth paraffin & flat champagne . names
written on blown up photos & dried Patrón nips .

       & if she were to scamper for crack caps
where no politician shows up for a photo op .

the swollen belly of the white addict
grows by the day .
police hesitate guessing the trimester .

Ꮭ ᏬᏗ Ꮤ ūsdii is Tsalagi for baby

her name is Anastasia . Margie her middle is . after your mother .

his name is Ryu . Kiyoshi her name is . his name is Chayton .

Nami her name is . his name is Hiroshi . Japanese for generous

her name Aroha . for love . Lightfoot her middle name is .

after your elogi . your aunt . Loki . Loki is hot . his name is Len .

hopi for flute . a lion's heart . Scandinavian .

      his middle name is Robert .

after your uncle . your edutsi . Mạ̈'ii her name is . coyote .

is Veda for eternal knowledge . Sanskrit . too many foreign films .

ain't feeling Kwanzaa . we won't name her Imani .

Yoruba is sooooo cliché . Hózhǫ́ . beauty . Mary her middle name is .

      after your aunt .

Ulutse . she arrived . she came . Ātaahua . beautiful . Elizabeth

is her middle name . his middle name is Joshua . after your grandfather .

after my great-grandfather . ududu . no one will be named after

your father . tu est pater . i willed this .

85

Miss Daisy lived in 2FW . she distilled water by boiling it .
she sprinkled ammonia outside her door to ward off evil spirits .
my first period took place in her bathroom .

her husband was a Pan-Africanist .
he spoke little . sold his Marcus Garvey flags & pins from his
green van outside the State Building .

the last tenant was a chain-smoker & filthy cat owner .
the real estate agent will only show you should you make   40x
the monthly rent in annual income . Zillow feels so lonely .
      HOA fees are depressing .

aged out . as in past ripe . the seeds roasted . wish it would each month .
SGAO⁰ those words make facts sting .

        "has your period stopped ?"

    crease in midriff reminds her of the last lyric . *i willed my moon*
spare her lord of hereditary titties . non-status titties . the app only serves
to monitor the moods . *turn off the Jeffrey Osborne & the Joan Osborne .*
she pours down the bowl no future from her DivaCup . Òtítọ́
won't carry the shakers ever . *i willed every tadpole to die* . lima bean .
    ain't a nickname for her own . won't name the nuthatch .
or her pothos . somewhere in there a possibility . was . or two .
   she wish it would each month . now wishes tali Shiba Inu .

        call me Kitsune

bless she a sesame . imagine for a second she envies propagating .
coulda woulda . this sure ain't antebellum . oh, what a sad purchase
she would have been . perhaps her genes ain't hearty . *i willed this ?*
   . perhaps every month when blood leaks the lining cries "nah.
  no . not again . not again ." vetiver root hangs on doorknob .

had i willed me sterile wanders in thought . a co-op has rules .

last winter here . at least the radiators are whistling . peri- too cold
& meno- too hot . this just ain't right . or it is .
   i will my cycle to return upon this residential closure .

          the end of woe is *a lie after all*
 . she wish it does each month . Ulutse . he named her Uluste .
daughter of men . she's arrived . clutching her Brut balm .
          prenatals are for thinning hair .

ᏗᎵᎫ diligu is Tsalagi for rice

sAquui siqua . one hog . corner tub . fatback .
kackaLack . pileated woodpeckers. daLala.
she drives .   into town You . lOg ceiling
b ea ms . exposed .   drives you . hawiya Ukayosv .
bacoN . cornEr tub . miss charlEne the name .
cook a mean rice & peas . sugar beans . turrets .
but   rice & peas the way you like . back in kackalacky .
h ere rice fielDs no more . To keep   company
someone . from tHe west indiEs . a big blAck mutt
a hound . breedIng in tupelo a war bleR . wrap around
porch . all new china . canadian geese come
 here all the Time . the ri ve r . tHe   sw am p bordEred by .
yAd kIn . jordan . wall to wall hardwood flooRs .
this muTt gonna k ee p tHE   cot ton mou ths
 f rom your chick ens . a r amp for yo u f or you a s coo tEr .

*inferno of 1992 . twentieth anniversary . "t.r.o.y." booms due to fitness
of recent rain drips . could be an automatic skylight . blocked
by prewar beams charred . save me a shower . heavy rain & climate change
& rolaids . won't he will .*

*the American cockroach on its back is said to be introduced to the Americas
thanks to the Atlantic slave trade. who knew?*

there is no field . there is no farm . no ticks to tweeze . no snapper
in bucket . no snapper to make soup .
no rice & liver . instead ponder the pain threshold .
inside dumbbell tenement . limestone & airy . hers is perhaps not
sensational enough for a headline . make pace for the stomp grounds .
   there is only an unkept cemetery . graves spread apart .
         some w/out gravestones.

ubi sunt sepculchra . one is under a tree . pleated are delusions . driving
in circles . the landscape changed . the sandbank traps those haunted .
the trap house stalks your ride . avoid the glances . want nothing .
ain't no sign of life but the pines . question . why return to this ?
what did she honestly expect ? what the estranged nephew said .
everyone is dead . the carolina gold comes from Fine Fare on 116th
& Lenox Foods forty years before . keep her wits . give she some sugar

god sent . the devil loves coprophages .
in around the corner someone had to know the family .
         newer faces now older residents .
bordered up are mysteries of the illegitimate . pained .
this toothless cousin . a hound stands guard on the porch .
SGAℓ° be grateful mommy went up north .
near the chipping walls . near drywall . by decline & memory blistered
         lips are zipped . any evidence long thrown in the trash .

Òtítọ́   there is an easier process .

study of roaches agonizing on the glue trap limb by limb escaping
or reckon w/ two free feel-ups the real estate agent took agency
over your calm demeanor & newfound inquiry into property taxes ,
            LLCs & gut renovations .

gratitude to the downy & red-bellied woodpeckers up north
like them . limbs are unglued .

> *"it's more to feed to your mind. Water, sun, & love,*
> *the one you love, all you need, the air you breathe."*

fantasma #2

coil & push. miss moccasin finds mommy. nearer to the
bank. a particular bank. muddy red deep. brown ruby
mud where catfish slide. & wallow she creeps. uncoils
adjusts her weight. the fork of her tongue. sniffs the air.
smells mommy's diaper. if there were diapers. smells
milk spilt. the hole in the nipple. too big to hold milk
in. if there were a bottle. her mouth whipping white.
like the cotton my great grandma picked. if she picked
like puffy pussy willows. like boiled bleached blouses.
no matter. she reaches. wraps around. breathes in
mommy. waits. the muscle does its constricting. does
she ever constrict?

close & afar. there's my great grandma. stocky. down
the bank. up the bank. tending to red mud. catfish in
the mud. her ankles coated by red mud. red like the eyes
of a black-crowned night heron w/ bait. not like salt
mines. more like socks. probably therapeutic. probably
not. catches dinner for two or three days.

my great grandma returns. skirt. or overalls. coated
w/ mud. the straw in her hat unwinds beneath the
sun. hot kacalak sun. forearms twisted chicken necks.
have handled a shotgun pretty good. have warned
male cousins of their wrongdoing to girls. have placed
shotguns in the faces of men. walks up to mommy.
says hello to miss moccasin. thanks her for keeping
eye on her grandbaby. thanks her for eating before she
came to work. thanks her for making sure no one else
came slithering over. she unwraps the snake. tosses her
aside politely. takes mommy & the catfish on home.
the snake. thorns thirsty. be's on her way.

where are your bones

"our beautiful flaw and terrible ornament."

Gwendolyn Brooks

ebo

                  to clean you para to wash hair

to untangle

        frotar feet

        rub your feet   para to oil

               to anoint *to curse you* to exercise

                  arms *to yank at your hair*

         to pinch your leg *to lotion your palms* to wash you

     to stroke head *to stain you to shame you* to feed

               feed your green & meyer

        lemon parakeets

     talk to them

   sing to them

               hold my tongue

   let the sister bitch *let the nephew bitch* let niece blame me the bitch

        blame anyone

   watch do nothing *like blind winos fondling pelagic fantasias*

   claim the liquor

       keep my ebo touch you everywhere *to abandon you*

     baby you **blame** you sleep *you* little victim *i*

quit my job & ***sostén mi lengua*** *hold my tongue*

        cautioned by elders *just be*

           a good daughter para

             am told am taught

             the

             good girl chores

   buy bye-bye panties

   blanched brand new bra from Lady Love   gloves usher ivory

why split your food stamps w/ someone who calls me a bitch on the regular

buy you socks *bought you a bed*
your food
                              rice & beans *camarón*
sweet plantains *california rolls*
beg you to eat *beg you to apologize*
                                        i listen
                              to your eyes rasp *to*
                              your finality curse
hear the fading   flee absent for one day *been weeks holding my tongue* always
                lying to you.

my first colonoscopy

they did not tell her it goes black :: memory :: dreams :: last words
language/s :: small talk over allergies :: & then :: a smirk of black
a question about travel :: brasil
  she arrives into the peat's gloom :: the decomposed ocean flutters

                  lonely :: here

   that descending device :: will she tear :: not easy to dish
dis at ease ish :: or clamp down on the ascensión

sole reference :: the chemo'ed colon of the mother
don't they hear the hassle :: *y'all don't love us like your calico bass*

          to prop mommy on a treadmill for stress test — post
          stroke — singing hypothesis cause surgeon's synopsis slept post;
          a shy evasive for the elderly — protect the white sturgeon
          at present but what about purebred beluga caviar —

they don't hear she tight   *not hatin' tight :: not weave tight*
not money tight :: not jean tight
                  not STD tight :: not EBT card tight :: not she say
                  he say they say what they say fuck they say fuck what they say
                  fish on tight fuck them all tight

said daughter's flight during said routine a decade-long
guilt trip :: said "routine"
w/ "small but real" risk :: what they previously said :: said that
guilt is something sinful :: though valid :: past incident
who's to blame on that vehicular assault :: third first fourth
fifth second resident ? didn't they see the oarfish beached

during 2006 tropical storms ?
   licensed medics too calm about flexible tubes up asses
for past tense there some past error
    daughter be mildly torn about getting guts torn
                       she tight

off w/ the costume just us wish this was euphoria the panic
loom attack on sins posthumous w/ Prozac hails like a wail Mary
hail Margie hail Margarite Martha hail Mahalia hail Mary O hell, Mary won't you?
when you found Jesus? near the Black Sea's basin we roam
Margaret's daughter Tasha's momma
the seismic cha cha high step deepens
moan about to crap
the barotrauma

sturdier her intestines :: can't Kunta-crip on bowel prep :: bentonite
spirituals & South African aloe :: cascara :: colonics :: sticky okra
she might aight :: or won't she :: bad genes can't glean elements
absent is w/in the human hymn :: silence is flax sinew & pig hide
soaking in a lukewarm chitterling bucket :: come :: they told me
who they :: they nothing :: no feeling :: nothing heard :: evade
reticulated pythons in the everglades w/ oaths break they water

                          or
                    salamanders

relapse mushroom ramen run off of white rice spam for pop tarts
low sodium says progresso won't go dannon run off of yoplait
down goes the milk of magnesia
instant nespresso solos some reflux of chicharrón cuchi cuchi
what falls out when they collapse
all day down the commode misfits
crap laci le beau

death ain't nothing but a fiber optic
a catheter :: *matrem et filia* :: absent
now is as they was :: is :: as
apart :: marred :: the gashed guts
crippled is the liquor-spawned

       & like mother :: the molting larva awakes
       from that blackening maalox murk
       someone's haze high on wormwood

       don't you pull me up so quickly
       i may get the bends

Evelyn "Champagne" King

a goddamn shame. ___ didn't go back to bury ___ own flesh & blood?

___ firstborn? ___ what? ain't have no money? who ___ people? well why

didn't ___ have any money? what ___ say? ___ evil as sin. ___ wouldn't give __

money for a bus ticket? __ going to hell. ___ gave __ money to go down

for ___ aunt's funeral but not ___ own daughter? lord. & what about ___

other two daughters? ain't neither of them can go? where her people?

ain't old enough to go on ___ own? why ___ ain't got no money?

where's the oldest? ___ did what to ___ firstborn? just left ___? ___ say ___

ain't raised ___? ___ aunt? well why ___ aunt ain't help ___ out? ___

dead too? who's in jail? pitiful. what about __? where's the rest of ___

people? what about ___ daughter's husband? can't the military help?

___ ain't got no other family to help? a ___ damn shame. me? __ ain't none

of my family. ___ gonna pay me back? mind my own damn business.

ain't none of my business. none of my business. no ma'am.

miss martha don't remember mommy's dead

dream pictures :: dream a painting on cardboard :: dream
youth :: how the older ones don't fade when lost for so long :: even
her disaster dreamt :: dream conversations w/ artists :: dream of
artists w/ aneurysms :: stunted tall walkie-talkie dreams :: *sueño*
impediments :: dream elegant older women & cosmetic
jewelry :: dream they keep the pictures :: dream they keep the
portraits of the dead :: dream storefronts :: dream Theaster & some
real shit about property & taxes & developers :: dream a Prada
endorsement or a vodka commercial in the guise of intellectual
discourses over inclusion & contemporary art :: dream the black mold
may avoid you :: dream dementia :: seizure dream :: dreamt The
Artist's deathbed is her bed is her first *real* bed is her *grown-ass woman*
bed is a full-size bed :: ain't even a *queen* :: dream next time a California
King if in the same household :: this time you save him :: dreamt a man
on Lexington dream :: dreamt lux cherry trees from Haiti :: dream
she found pictures of Mommy as a girl :: dreamt decades ago :: dream
she wasn't that bad a visual artist :: dream tags & cardboard :: more
cardboard :: *pangarap* a demolition :: *ale* the dead almond
sapling :: *sonhe* in the rain :: soaked kicks :: the labyrinth dreaming
dreams balding, dreaded men :: dream an open-heart surgery :: dream
you died :: she died :: dream Spotified commercials :: later
she survived :: dreamt the mother's fibroid on CT scan :: dreamt
the scar down her chest :: the scar paraded dreams :: dream
floaters :: *asgitisdi* :: dream plaster & drywall come tumbling
down :: dream no one remembers these transom shadows :: dream
somewhere else :: elsewhere :: anywhere :: not here

kummerspeck

bacon letter to the darkening land:

plaster calamine pink between groovy meat . everything's
like a ritual . you pardon chubby cheeks & think of mommy . growing
into hers . the gravy is sweet & your tummy hangs . the fuck . no ash in
summer . johnson & johnson . powder rites . so . we come to this . our
alignment five floors up . a larger cup . bunker & cave . magic garden

of inedible zz's .
       cacti . devil's ivy .

look . our hüftgold similarly weighted .
               rolling twin entenmann's pound smack trap.

sigh . bad genes . bluntly . it's the hips that go first . once a year . no
not puckering . that bubble-neck hump . a slice of spam . you
buy the venison version . once a year . low sodium . vienna sausages not
available in Virginia . cussin' corona . rolling over ain't funny . afraid
it be normalized . that you'd adapt to the weight . never favored . had to
come from yo' daddy . you so miracle whip . when all of her disappear

this ain't a body shame . more a *mommy* shame . hot sizzling potpie . you
cut an eye at dimples . discoloration in gaps . no need to see your toenails
how you favor in months . this nose never been broken . gots no history
of battery . pure potlikker . prefer butter over country crock . admit
you vomit now once a week . the crunch of anniversary bacon is rapture

know baby powder brings back the dead . you meant to bury defeat . that
bazooka gum . your pound cake . yellow grits just white grits . whether it's
bob's or quaker . our savory rettungsring . coarse & haunted

               don't you look like she?

cliff notes

man is patient. *i have* heard of morgues. how they lose
bodies. bodies never picked up. the estranged unclaimed. or
mismatched bracelets. or toe tags. never a dull school trip
until now. he convinces me. his eyes do. *is he a father or a
husband?* he assures w/ his tongue. *please don't let him become
impatient.* the morgue is not at capacity. yet. *for now.* says will
work w/ families. *please don't let him make me mute.* was told
about the impatience of coroners. of their need to find space.
what might he speculate of this family? the kind w/ no life insurance.
to make money on vacancies. what hospitals make money on
beds. *they do say if you wanna die go to Mount Sinai.* i have heard
nightmares. missing spouses. was in a church when they found
one behind the church on 123rd & Garvey Park. bodies buried
in vacant lots. landfills off the coast of Mannahatta. or bloating
while a family handles the paperwork in Mexico. *'tis illegal to
bury the dead in Central Park. before i knew that, i buried my last
cat there as mommy had buried the two before.* rotting from bad
refrigeration. or they were left too long. no one claimed them.
where is potter's field? does Hart Island have vacancies? the
stuff Rikers lifers shovel & quicklime. the last bedsheet. for
what i have. don't. *mommy did* put money on a plot in Peekskill.
i need not cry. no turkey buzzards in Harlem. so work w/ him.
rearrange. InstaVet's crematory rates are by the pound.

the orphan is becoming a refugee. trust.

kombucha

*

at first, pacifier/less. a thumb offers most. the heart tremors among
the first beating. in Paris, i bathed w/ naked women
wrinkled & tart. the heavy postwar memory of fossilized sinks. who
hides beneath mosaic & tadelakt chipped? i am here to love me. cursed
haunch & dimpled bottom. scrub me spoiled w/ loofah till their
arms tire. my skin, a bright pink cashew refuted by the hearts
of sons. am i, the only lonely, in this hammam cast out?
commandments & confirmations. haven't we all been soured?
honor thy father, mother, thy suitor, lover, thy wedded; themselves
foolish. foolish me w/ dreams. somehow the movers were never
booked. bellies never swollen pearls. in former lives i was all brides.

*

grandmothers rub away who wronged me. three wishes ambered. brides
don't keep dirty kitchens. toes flinch as the Korean woman files. never
had my feet been tended to. never had anyone present themselves
as example. the hammam was peaceful. Oakland's mani-pedi busy. soured
pearls roll off my forehead. doused cheeks clipped nails. teach me? step out
foot soak spoiled. ask for ten minutes more. kneading needs. opened heart.
i shrink inside the steamed seasoned. slurp pineapple tea. pause. my
heels absent callus. shoulders oiled. almond & olive soap. nursed & cursed
few. in a reoccurring dream, from mommy's skull, a flab of flesh she who
cared less for stiff neck or gouty ankles. legion of poor unpolished women.
dull moments. faint blood drifts past one vessel. what secrets am i among?

*

once we lived in a railroad tenement. have dreamt my mommy's death among
mothers down the block. the shells say to rub her hands like the working women
we never afforded. lotion forearms that work menthol into a sibling's chest. who
on the other side of the curtain? as elbow pressed against shoulder blade, i cursed
myself for prolonging sores spent on frivolous leisure. all guilt up. water's weak.
every knot of muscle is as callused as the heart. tearing nerves cry out.
mommy, only mommy scratched my back. why olive branches never soured
thrashed against the flesh that now sags. into the cold pool i go. the Russians
immune to steam & hot rocks. is how one releases daytime stories. so simple
a late bloom or late loving studies. these are the rituals of the unanointed.

*

i am the daughter of men. i am the last offspring fathered
by a numbers runner. apparently. among
whisperers, gated windows hurried to clear wax out the ears of women.
ratchet-ass blue jays perched on stoops. stop & stare at this child. who
she favor? Frankie the I-talian or the *Porto Riccun*? the Jew?
didn't even know his true name to be Marion. mommy cursed
the gossip w/ a pinch of snuff, bottom lip tucked. black spit marks their
paths. cross. break backs. daughter of cotton pickers & Newports.
hearts fatty on liquor & crackling salt pork. afterbirth soaks into the grout.
see? this here? this where i popped out of mommy.
the latter contraction came late. thought i was a cramp.
what to do w/ sitting water? sour limestone useless for a cradleboard.
birth. oh my. what did they, women, daughters of men
swaddle me w/ that afternoon? what was the weather?
she never felt it? too numbed by spirits? by daughters? by the unwed?

*

the encounter says i am smooth like a baby & butter
that i am a fire hydrant's valve flushed opened
the sag of my tit slinks into a second's gap between us
where made noticeble, the morning after, is the trace
of a saftig body & scent from earlier that day.
i won't mind it. it's not for commentary.
the craft of indifference. what is mine.
what i don't own. how dare. the nerve.
his mouth. the stench of tobacco. i caution, implore toothpaste
to get the night on.
his chest is silverback flypaper. is that cold for a descriptor?
Murdock & Marvin. what a duet that would have been.
an osprey overhead carries an unlikely meal. some garden snake. & the sky
shifts from rainbow marble to shears of Pantone 15-4020.
in the clouds a daughter dreams me. a "plump fine chanteuse."
relaxed. spooned & selfish.

111th Gothic

Miss Simmons · o que você vê nelas · Mr. Tracy's daughters

Miss Scott · as palavras na carta são tuas · Prisha · hózhǫ · Mary · Kaprice

Miss Janet · Miss Cat · Miss Gloria

Hózhǫ si gedoa' · você sabe fazer chover · Nora · Miss Pearl · her aunt · Não somos daqui · her name was Chucky · Miss Josie Brown

Cassie · Chucky · Debbie & Jesse Gray

Helen · Staysha · her sister · Miss Josie · Gwen & Madeline

aunt · Miss Audrey

Miss Perry · Peanut · quero ir para casa · they are sisters · her daughters

Bosco · Keisha · aí vem ela · Yvette · Miss Sue · Erika

Mary Epps · Pat · Lisa

April June · Antonia aka Toni · eu não tenho netos · Puerto Rican Denise · Mrs Margaret Brown

Miss Minnie · Kivyette · Miss Cora · Miss Lulu · Sandra · Miss Lydia

her daughter · Shaniqua · Vivian · Necee · preciso dormir · Tiny · Sonia

Melvina. · mother · Denise · Knuata's wife Gwen · Sharon · Shaniqua Antonia aka Toni · Puerto Rican Pat · Miss Ruth · Melissa · my sister · Miss Sharon

Michelle Daniels · Veronica · Gigi · Mrs. Vargas · Carmen · Elizabeth · Tina

Nelvinna · Madeline · Miss Daniels · Ronnie · Angie · Emily Vargas · Miss Margaret

never secure in the long mourning texture

   black mold gets at you

and then, from an actual dream

                *dips stella d'oro into sanka

         who's voice shattered the glass ?   is mommy's forehead a sinkhole ?

      is a long hallway . the sun through living room transom facing south .

      indirect light good for mother-in-law's tongue .

             . 144 across from 141 .

      two spaces merge . both on fifth floors .

      railroads postwar . peach swine tile . mommy . always leaning

        over the deep kitchen sink . always older . thy memorex we interrogate .

      precision . deep double sinks . enameled stained & chipped .

        the weathered gauze across her forehead . it falls . always falls .

           the skin   falls . from underneath flaps open .

      always into the sink & out blood . spills vomit . always like vomit

   why you put your sinkhole out here in the street

                  like the way rotten eggs soar out sidewalk garbage

"items of confectionery"

am not	Black enough
am not	an enrolled tribal member
am not	older than sixty
am not	younger than thirty
am not	Native enough
do not	have a White parent
am not	White passing
	or White presenting
am not	1/32
am not	Harlem enough
am not	a resident of Community Board 11
am not	ghetto enough
am not	Southern enough
am not	a recovering addict
am not	Caribbean
am not	fluent in Spanish
am not	fluent in English
am not	w/ an obvious Spanish-sounding surname
though	my middle name is suspect
don't	have a descendent on the Dawes Rolls,
	the Guion Miller Roll, the Henderson Roll,
	the Baker Roll, the Mullay Rolls,
	the Echota Rolls . . . wait. do I?
don't	write about my hair texture
don't	write about skin color
am not	emerging
am not	categorically LatinxLatinaHispanicSpanish
am not	Afro — Afro — Afro — Afro —
am not	formally incarcerated
am	often consulted never compensated
am	w/out a mother
am not	an orphan
am not	a single mother
am not	a mother
am	no mother

hour of the star

the time is 11 p.m., _____ was born alive

the time is 8:44 a.m., _____ the mother can read & can write

the time is 7:32 p.m., _____ the father is unknown

the time is 5:21 p.m., the infant has been given eye drops at the time of birth

the time is 12:37 a.m., the mother's race is Colored

the time is 4:49 a.m., the name for the child will be decided by a nurse

as the mother is high on Twilight

as the mother's grandfather died in a sanatorium somewhere near Pee Dee

the time is 7:49 a.m., the name for the child will be decided by a nurse

as the mother was under the influence of alcohol at the time of her arrival

as the mother thought the child to be a boy

the time is 5:38 p.m., the mother's residence is unknown

the time is 3:22 p.m., the mother's occupation is field hand

the time is 6:14 a.m., the child is alive

personal & artistic inventory

B. V. S.—Form 16

North Carolina State Board of Health
BUREAU OF VITAL STATISTICS

12

STANDARD CERTIFICATE OF BIRTH

1. PLACE OF BIRTH		
County Anson	Registration District No. _____	Certificate No. **19**
Township Lilesville	or Village _____	or
City _____ (No. _____)	(If birth occurred in hospital or institution, give its name instead of street and number)	St. _____ Ward)

2. FULL NAME OF CHILD Margaret Elizabeth Diggs *(If child is not yet named, make supplemental report, as directed)*

3. Sex of child Female	To be answered only in event of plural births.	4. Twin, triplet, or other _____	6. Parents married? No	7. Date of birth March 28–32
		5. Number, in order of birth _____		(Name of Month) (Day) (Year)

8. FATHER	14. MOTHER
Full name Unknown	Full maiden name Margie Diggs 2 00
9. Residence (Usual place of abode) If nonresident, give place and State	15. Residence (Usual place of abode) If nonresident, give place and State Pee Dee
10. Color or race _____ 11. Age at last birthday _____ (Years)	16. Color or race Col 17. Age at last birthday 18 (Years)
12. Birthplace (city or place) _____ (State or country)	18. Birthplace (city or place) _____ (State or country) Anson County
13. Occupation _____ Nature of industry _____	19. Occupation _____ Nature of industry Farm hand

20. Number of children of this mother (Taken as of time of birth of child herein certified and including this child.)	(a) Born alive and now living _____	(b) Born alive, but now dead 0	(c) Stillborn 0

21. Did you use drops in baby's eyes at birth to prevent blindness? **Yes** If not, why not? _____

CERTIFICATE OF ATTENDING PHYSICIAN OR MIDWIFE*

22. I hereby certify that I attended the birth of this child, who was **born alive** at **8 P.M.** on the date above stated.
(born alive or stillborn) (Hour, a.m. or p.m.)

23. (Signature) X *Eliza Robinson*
(State whether _____ or midwife)

24. P.O. Pee Dee

25. Witness *J. L. Wyatt*
(Signature of witness necessary only when 23 is signed by mark)

Given name added from supplemental report

Amended 9-13 1982
_____ Registrar

26. Filed **4-7-32** 19___ by *J. L. Wyatt*
Local Registrar

28 P.O. Lilesville

*When there was no attending physician or midwife, then the father, householder, etc., should make this return. If a child breathes even once, it must not be reported as stillborn. No report is desired of stillbirths before the fifth month of pregnancy.

LDSS-3621 NYC (Rev. 2/03)   FS Red/Clos/Cont-A/C-Adequate

NOTICE OF INTENT TO CHANGE FOOD STAMP BENEFITS (Adequate Only)(NYC)

NOTICE DATE:	7|7|05	NAME AND ADDRESS OF AGENCY CENTER OR DISTRICT OFFICE

CASE NUMBER ▮▮▮▮   CIN NUMBER ▮▮▮▮

F-63 HOMEBOUND CENTER   F-63 HOME BOUND CTR.
215 DUFFIELD STREET 3rd Fl   SERVICE UNIT
BROOKLYN, NEW YORK 1120▮   ▮▮▮▮

CASE NAME (And C/O Name if Present) AND ADDRESS

Margaret Diggs
NY NY 10025

GENERAL TELEPHONE NO. FOR
QUESTIONS OR HELP

OR   Agency Conference   (718) 237-7520

Fair Hearing information
and assistance

Record Access   F-63 HOME BOUND CTR.
SERVICE UNIT
Legal Assistance   ▮18-237-7576 7577

OFFICE F-63   F 3?   WORKER NO.   UNIT OR WORKER (18)

We are CHANGING your Food Stamp Benefits, as explained below next to the checked boxes ☑

FOOD STAMP BENEFITS NOT PICKED UP WITHIN 270 DAYS CANNOT BE REPLACED

1. ☑ **INCREASE** your Food Stamp Benefits from $ _____ 44.00 _____ to $ _____ 134.00 _____
   effective _____

   ☐ Your Food Stamp Benefits certification period has been extended. Your benefits will now end in
   _____

2. ☐ **CONTINUE** your Food Stamp Benefits at $ _____ effective _____

   ☐ Your Food Stamp Benefits certification period has been extended. Your benefits will now end in
   _____

3. ☐ **REDUCE** your Food Stamp Benefits from $ _____ to $ _____
   effective _____

   ☐ Your Food Stamp Benefits certification period has been extended. Your benefits will now end in
   _____

4. ☐ **DISCONTINUE** your Food Stamp Benefits as of _____

5. ☐ **OVERPAYMENT INFORMATION**

   ☐ We are establishing a Food Stamp Benefits overpayment because you or your household got more in
   Food Stamp Benefits than you should have. See the Demand Letter and also, if your case is closing,
   the Repayment Agreement for more information on this overpayment. **This decision is base on 18
   NYCRR 387.19.**

   ☐ You currently have a Food Stamp Benefits overpayment. If your case is closing, see the Demand Letter
   and Repayment Agreement for more information on the amount you owe and how you will repay this
   overpayment.

   ☐ The benefit above reflects a ____% reduction (recoupment) of $ _____ in your benefits in
   order to repay your overpayment. **This decision is based on 18 NYCRR 387.19.**

6. ☐ If you are getting Public Assistance and/or Medical Assistance, this change will NOT affect those benefits.

The reason for this action is: Agency Rebudgated Your Case To Reflect The
Brown Utility Standard. See Line 19/ on budget.

P.O. BOX 02-9121
BROOKLYN GPO
BROOKLYN, N.Y. 11202-9121

The City of New York

HUMAN RESOURCES ADMINISTRATION
FAMILY INDEPENDENCE ADMINISTRATION

CONFERENCE PHONE 718-237-7576
NUMERO PARA CONFERENCIA

DIGGS MARGARET

MANHATTAN   NY 10025

IMC/FSO :
CASE   :
CLI   :

FAM SIZE: 1
DATE   :   12/04/2005

NOTICE OF INTENT TO REDUCE FOOD STAMP BENEFITS
AVISO DE INTENCION DE REDUCIR SUS BENEFICIOS DE CUPONES DE ALIMENTOS

DEAR SIR/MADAM:

THIS IS TO INFORM YOU THAT WE INTEND TO REDUCE YOUR FOOD STAMP BENEFITS EFFECTIVE JANUARY 1, 2006 FOR THE FOLLOWING REASON:

BEGINNING JANUARY 2006, SOCIAL SECURITY, SSI AND/OR VETERAN'S BENEFITS WILL INCREASE BY 4.1%. IF YOU ARE IN RECEIPT OF ANY OF THESE FEDERAL BENEFITS, THIS INCREASE IN INCOME TO YOUR HOUSEHOLD MUST BE CONSIDERED IN DETERMINING YOUR FOOD STAMP BENEFIT LEVEL. IF YOU ARE IN RECEIPT OF BOTH SOCIAL SECURITY BENEFITS AND SSI, YOUR JANUARY SSI BENEFITS WILL BE REDUCED BY THE AMOUNT OF YOUR SOCIAL SECURITY BENEFIT INCREASE. THESE INCOME CHANGES MUST ALSO BE CONSIDERED IN DETERMINING YOUR FOOD STAMP BENEFITS. HOWEVER, THE AMOUNT OF THE FOOD STAMP REDUCTION WILL NOT NECESSARILY BE A DOLLAR FOR DOLLAR REDUCTION OF FOOD STAMP BENEFITS.

IF YOU ARE AN SSI RECIPIENT LIVING ALONE IN THE COMMUNITY WHO IS PARTICIPATING IN THE NEW YORK STATE NUTRITION IMPROVEMENT PROJECT (NYSNIP), AND YOU WERE RECEIVING $109 PER MONTH IN FOOD STAMP BENEFITS, BEGINNING IN JANUARY 2006 YOU WILL RECEIVE $100 PER MONTH. IF YOU WERE RECEIVING $102 PER MONTH IN FOOD STAMP BENEFITS, BEGINNING IN JANUARY 2006 YOU WILL RECEIVE $93 PER MONTH AS STATED ABOVE. THIS REDUCTION IN YOUR FOOD STAMP GRANT IS DUE TO THE INCREASE IN YOUR FEDERAL BENEFITS.

PAGE 2 OF THIS NOTICE IS A FINANCIAL FACT SHEET WHICH SHOWS YOUR NEW FOOD STAMP BENEFIT AMOUNT AND ALL THE INCOME INFORMATION ON OUR COMPUTER FILE THAT WAS USED TO CALCULATE YOUR NEW FOOD STAMP BENEFIT. WE HAVE ENCLOSED BUDGET WORKSHEETS WHICH YOU CAN USE TO DETERMINE WHETHER WE HAVE CORRECTLY DETERMINED YOUR NET FOOD STAMP INCOME. SEE 18 NYCRR 387.10, 387.12 AND 387.15.

QUEREMOS INFORMARLE DE LA INTENCION DE REDUCIR SUS BENEFICIOS DE CUPONES DE ALIMENTOS A SER EFECTIVO DEL 1 DE ENERO DE 2006 POR LAS RAZON ENUMERADAS ABAJO:

COMENZANDO EN ENERO DE 2006 LOS BENEFICIOS DE SEGURO SOCIAL, SSI Y/O BENEFICIOS DE VETERANOS SERAN AUMENTADOS POR LA CANTIDAD DE 4.1%. SI USTED RECIBE CUALQUIERA DE ESTOS BENEFICIOS FEDERALES, ESTE AUMENTO EN EL INGRESO DE SU HOGAR DEBE SER CONSIDERADO EN LA CALCULACION DEL NIVEL DE SUS BENEFICIOS DE CUPONES DE ALIMENTOS. SI USTED RECIBE BENEFICIOS DE SEGURO SOCIAL Y SSI, SU BENEFICIO DE SSI EN ENERO SERA REDUCIDO POR LA CANTIDAD DEL AUMENTO EN SU BENEFICIO DE SEGURO SOCIAL. ESTOS CAMBIOS EN INGRESO DEBEN SER CONSIDERADOS EN LA CALCULACION DE SUS BENEFICIOS DE CUPONES DE ALIMENTOS. SIN EMBARGO, LA CANTIDAD DE LA REDUCCION DE SUS CUPONES DE ALIMENTOS NO SERA NECESARIAMENTE UNA REDUCCION DE UN DOLAR POR CADA DOLAR DE SUS BENEFICIOS DE CUPONES DE ALIMENTOS.

SI USTED ES UN BENEFICIARIO DE SSI QUE VIVE SOLO(A) EN LA COMUNIDAD Y PARTICIPA EN EL PROYECTO DEL ESTADO DE NUEVA YORK PARA UNA MEJOR NUTRICION (NYSNIP - POR SUS SIGLAS EN INGLES), Y RECIBE $109 AL MES EN BENEFICIOS DE CUPONES PARA ALIMENTOS, COMENZANDO EN ENERO DEL 2006 USTED RECIBIRA $100 AL MES. SI USTED RECIBIA $102 AL MES EN CUPONES, COMENZANDO EN ENERO DEL 2006, USTED RECIBIRA $93 AL MES. TAL COMO SE LE INDICO ANTERIORMENTE, ESTA REDUCCION EN EL SUBSIDIO DE CUPONES SE DEBE AL INCREMENTO EN SUS BENEFICIOS FEDERALES.

LA PAGINA DOS DE ESTE AVISO ES UNA HOJA DE DATOS FINANCIEROS QUE MUESTRA SU NUEVA CANTIDAD DE BENEFICIOS DE CUPONES DE ALIMENTOS Y TODA LA INFORMACION SOBRE SUS INGRESOS EN NUESTRO ARCHIVO COMPUTA RIZADO UTILIZADO PARA CALCULAR SU NUEVO BENEFICIO DE CUPONES DE ALIMENTOS.
INCLUIDO ES UNA HOJA DE PRESUPUESTO LA CUAL USTED PUEDE UTILIZAR PARA DETERMINAR SI HEMOS CALCULADO CORRECTAMENTE SU INGRESO NETO PARA CUPONES DE ALIMENTOS. VEA LAS REGULACIONES 387.10, 387.12 Y 387.15.

SINCERELY,
ATENTAMENTE,

SETH DIAMOND, EXECUTIVE DEPUTY COMMISSIONER
FAMILY INDEPENDENCE ADMINISTRATION

30585

XL0263 (11/05)

Margret Diggs

V. ADDITIONAL COMMENTS

Describe any other aspects of the patient's medical, social, family or home situation which affects the patient's ability to function, or may affect need for home care.

Ms. Diggs is a 70 y.o. single, retired woman who lives alone in an Adequate Apartment and is maintained by Social Security / SSR, Miene + M/caid. Pt. suffers from multiple medical problems, and diagnosed End Stage Renal Disease 2° Hypertension °/o CAD °/o MI ° 1992 + 1998. Ms Diggs commenced receiving chronic hemodialysis 3x weekly + 4 hours on MWF III; and adheres to overall treatment regimen.

Ms. Diggs recently underwent a series of medical problems and reports a physical change in level of functioning. Ms. Diggs experienced a cardiac arrest, was resuscitated and suffered an In-Pt hospitalization, commencing in the ER + CCU. Pt. has a Pace-maker implant - which regulates pts cardiac condition - and now required to remain active within limited constraints.

Given the above, we are requesting a change in Ms. Diggs home care services. Ms. Diggs change in cardiac condition results in limitations of excess exertion - lifting, reaching, walking + reduce palpitations, breathlessness. We are consequently requesting a change from 3 hours 3x week to 5 hours 5 days a week to maintain pt in community environs with reduced risk factors.

If further information is needed, please feel free to recontact us.

Thanks,
Lynnette ███████████

Signature of Person Completing Additional Comments Section	Title Social Worker	Date March 3rd 03
Lynnette Ortiz ACSW	Agency Mt. Sinai Dialysis Center	

120

margaret diggs
itf LATASHA DIGGS

ACCOUNT No.

	DATE	WITHDRAWALS	DEPOSITS	INTEREST	BALANCE	TRANS.
1						
2	08/09/99	25.00			1.02*	615
3	08/31/99	1.02			0.00*	615
4	08/31/99		0.01		0.01*	615
5	09/01/99		356.96		356.97*	615
6	09/01/99	330.00			26.97*	615
7						
8	09/03/99		186.00		212.97	
9						
10	09/03/99	186.00			26.97	
11	09/23/99	15.00			11.97	
12	09/30/99		.04		12.0	
13						
14	10/01/99		356.96		363.97	
15	10/01/99		186.00		549.97	
16	10/01/99	356.00			193.97	614
17						
18						
19	10/02/99	176.00			17.97	
20	10/18/99	13.00			4.97	
21	10/29/99		.04		5.01	
22	10/29/99	4.97			.04	
23	11/01/99		356.96		357.00	
24	11/01/99	356.00			1.00	

BANCO POPULAR
MEMBER FEDERAL RESERVE SYSTEM
INSURED BY FDIC

121

The Mount Sinai Medical Center

The Mount Sinai Hospital
Mount Sinai School of Medicine

One Gustave L. Levy Place
New York, NY 10029–6574

Date: 8-31-98

Re: Housing

To Whom It May Concern:

Margaret Diggs is a patient at the Mount Sinai Dialysis Center. She/He is diagnosed with End Stage Renal Disease secondary to Hypertension, and must receive life sustaining chronic hemodialysis treatments 3 times weekly for approximately 3 to 4 hours. She/He is frequently debilitated with symptoms of chronic fatigue, muscle cramping and weakness, nausea, vomiting, dizziness, shortness of breath, and blood pressure irregularities. She/He must follow a specific dietary regime, restrict fluids and take medication on a regular basis. As a result, Ms. Diggs would benefit from an apt. in an elevator building. Her/His primary physician is Dr. R. Stein, MD who can be reached at (212) 241-4060. If I can be of further assistance, please feel free to contact me at (212) 987-7597.

Sincerely,

Elena Filetger, CSW

122

The City of New York

HUMAN RESOURCES ADMINISTRATION
MEDICAL ASSISTANCE PROGRAM

IMPORTANT
NOTICE OF DENIAL OF YOUR MEDICAL ASSISTANCE APPLICATION

┌ Mrs. LaTasha Diggs. ┐
14-11 W 111 St, Apt. 5RE
└ NY, NY, 10026 ┘

DATE: _04 07 97_

CASE NUMBER: ███████████

HOSPITAL ADMISSION DATE: _01 18 97_

GENERAL INFORMATION TEL. #: 1-718-291-1900

WE ARE SENDING YOU THIS NOTICE TO TELL YOU THAT THE MEDICAL ASSISTANCE PROGRAM WILL:

☐ - DENY - your Medicaid application because:

CODE	TEXT
202	YOU ARE BETWEEN TWENTY-ONE AND SIXTY-FOUR YEARS OF AGE AND ARE NOT DISABLED OR BLIND. YOUR MONTHLY INCOME OF $ _431.76_ EXCEEDS THE PUBLIC ASSISTANCE STANDARD OF NEED WHICH IS $ _352.10_ BY $ _79.66_. REPEAL OF SSL366 (2) (c). 18 NYCRR 360.3 (c), 360.28, 360.31, PART 352.

☐ - TAKE NO ACTION - on your Medicaid application since it was withdrawn at the request of: _____
_____

The law or regulation which allows us to do this is: _____

Dm. Brownfain ███ ███ ███
Worker   Title   Section   Division

YOU HAVE THE RIGHT TO APPEAL THIS DECISION

We will review this decision with you if you call us at 1-212-630-0996 and ask for a **LOCAL CONFERENCE**. You also have the right to ask for a **STATE FAIR HEARING**. You must request a **STATE FAIR HEARING** within 60 days of the date on the top of this Notice. You must meet this deadline to request a **STATE FAIR HEARING** even if you ask for a **LOCAL CONFERENCE** first. The **STATE FAIR HEARING** is held by the New York State Department of Social Services.

BE SURE TO READ THE ENCLOSED NOTICE ON HOW TO APPEAL THIS DECISION

(vea al dorso)

MAP 2087A (face)
(rev. 4/21/93)

123

Latasha Diggs

C.D. Middle Class Exam*

s.Tollinchi and Mr.Colón

.me:

66%

90.5%

Nov.16,1983

Chapters 1&2

ART I:

Use the following words to complete the sentences below.

talking	Christians	strength	yourself	taking
people	heart	caring	mind	speaking
Mickey Mouse	goal	neighbor	soul	team
hate	records	saints	Joan Jett	paper
loving	special	reason	love	I Love You
Mr.Colon	building	together	Jesus	hello

1.Prayer is a way of _talking_ to God.

2.The church consist of the _people_ in it not the _building_ itself.

3.A COMMUNITY is a special group of people working _together_ for a special _reason_ or for a special _team_.

4.If we _love_ each other as _Jesus_ loves us then the world will know we are _together_.

5.We can be Jesus' friends forever by...

"Love the Lord your God with all your _heart_, with all your _soul_, with all your _love_, and with all your mind. Love your _neighbor_ as _yourself_."

'.Love is _caring_ for your family, community, teachers, friends, hobbies, nature, and God. It means _Jesus_ care of others' things. Love is also _people_ those you hate. It means speaking to one another.

rtII:

Answer the following questions.

1.Name some communities you belong to.   C

Girl Scouts, Science Reserch Training program, the church.

2.Are we the Religious Instruction class a community? Why or why not?

Yes, It is because we are a group of people working together and we shares things with one another.   C

5. How do you know that Jesus is your friend?

Well, he gave his life for us and he cares for us and he tell us to be with one another.

6. What are some ways we can be friends to those in our community?

Share things with people, make people feel better when they are blue - care for them, play with them and love them

BONUS!!!!!!!!!!!

Spell the religious instructor's last name backwards.(the female one)

IHCNILLOT .SM

a kind of selective glossary

9e7ba, Qehbaor, Kehba is the Arabic (or Aribaci) equivalent to the word
  "Ho" or "Whore."
ᎠᎨᏳᏣ (agehutsa): daughter (Tsalagi)
ᎠᏂᎨᏳᏣ (anigehutsa): daughters (Tsalagi)
ᎢᏩᎩᎸ (vgilv): my sister (Tsalagi)
ᎠᎩᏚᏓ (ageduda): my grandfather (Tsalagi)
ᏅᏓ (nvda): sun or moon (Tsalagi)
ᎡᎵᏏ (elisi): grandmother (Tsalagi)
ᏍᎦᏃᎹ: truth (Tsalagi)
ᏍᎵᎧᏍ (galitsode): house (Tsalagi)
ᎡᎶᎩ (elogi): aunt
ᎤᎶᎩ (ulogi): her aunt
ageyutsa: girl (Tsalagi)
agigohniyoga: I am late (Tsalagi)
ahani gedoa: I am here; here I am (Tsalagi)
ahani ūsdi edoa: the baby is here (Tsalagi)
aí vem ela: Here she comes (Portuguese)
ale: and (Tsalagi)
anidalonige: Asians; literal translation, yellow people (Tsalagi)
aonde você vai?: Where do you go? (Portuguese)
as palavras na carta são tuas: the words in the letter are yours (Portuguese)
asgitisdi: dream (Tsalagi)
ascensión (Spanish)
ayotli or *ayohli*: offspring; child (Tsalagi)
ch'aqey: to throw stones; to throw rocks (Quechua)
CPS: Child Protective Services
dalala: woodpecker (Tsalagi)
dali ela vai para casa: from there she goes home (Portuguese)
degvdanilvgi: I am accepting you (Tsalagi)
diligu: rice (Tsalagi)
dvgedoli: I am going to come back (Tsalagi)
ebo: offering; sacrifice (Yoruba)

eduda: grandfather (my) (Tsalagi)

elisi: grandmother (my) (Tsalagi)

estou doente: I am sick (Portuguese)

etsi nuwahnisadi: mom is responsible for me being here (Tsalagi)

eu cuido de você: I look after you (Portuguese)

eu amo a minha mamãe: I love my mommy (Portuguese)

eu não tenho netos: I don't have grandchildren (Portuguese)

eu não quero pensar: I don't want to think (Portuguese)

eu vou esperar: I will wait. (Portuguese)

eu vou esperar para ver o que vai acontecer: I will wait to see what will happen (Portuguese)

frotar: rub (Spanish)

goligi: I understood (Tsalagi)

hawiya ukayosv: bacon (Tsalagi)

hilvsgi tsataga: chickens (Tsalagi)

hla osda yaquadanvta: I do not feel good (Tsalagi)

HOA: Homeowners Association

hózhǫ́: beauty (Diné)

hózhoǫ́áhásdlį́į́': there is beauty again (Diné)

hüftgold: hip gold (German)

IRT: Interborough Rapid Transit Company

kackalacky, *kakalak*, *cackalacka*: The Carolinas

kummerspeck: grief fat or its literal meaning: grief bacon (German).

matrem et filia: mother and daughter (Latin)

milonga: often associated from the dance form Tango, as explained by Dr. Robert Farris Thompson on AfroPop's "A Tango with Robert Farris Thompson," milonga means messages of defiance, an argument, or even lawsuit

Não somos daquí: We are not from here (Portuguese)

nelagi: let it alone; let it be (Tsalagi)

nuna phiña: angry spirit (Quechua)

NYCHA: New York City Housing Authority

o que você vê nelas: What do you see in them? (Portuguese)

orina de oro: urine gold (Spanish)

Òtítọ́: truth (Yoruba)

pangarap: dreams (Tagalog)

preciso dormir: I need to sleep (Portuguese)

primum non nocere: first, do no harm (Latin)

quero ir para casa: I want to go home (Portuguese)

rani mrida: I am ill; I am not emotionally well (Arabic)

rettungsring: lifebelt or love handles (German)

saquui siqua: one hog (Tsalagi)

sim, eu não tenho um bebé: Yes, I do not have a child (Portuguese)

schtick: gimmick (Yiddish)

shiyaagi hózhǫ́: there is beauty below me (Diné)

si gedoa: I am still here (Tsalagi)

sonhe: to dream (Portuguese)

sostén mi lengua: hold my tongue (Spanish)

SSI: Supplemental Security Income

tadelakt: wall surfacing technique used in Moroccan architecture to
   waterproof. It is composed of black soap, olives, and lime plaster.

THOT: That Hoe Over There

tsaduliha: you were saying (Tsalagi)

tsigatiya: I am waiting (Tsalagi)

tsulisdanala: catfish (Tsalagi)

ugama: soup (Tsalagi)

ubi sunt sepulchra: where are the graves? (Latin)

uksdaha: oops; my mistake (Tsalagi)

usdi: small (Tsalagi)

ūsdii: baby (Tsalagi)

uweyv or *equoni*: river / creek (Tsalagi)

uweyvi: meander

você sabe fazer chover: Do you know how to make it rain? (Portuguese)

vou tentar: I will try (Portuguese)

zaftig: voluptuous (Yiddish); coming from the German word saftig for
   "juicy."

"natasha is going to kill boris" contains a quote from the movie *Avengers: Age of Ultron*.

"eu vou esperar . . ." contains lyrics from Peter Gabriel "Shock the Monkey" & Kendrick Lamar "How Much a Dollar Cost."

"cling" is a golden shovel based on the line "Child with continuing cling issue his No in final fire," written by Gwendolyn Brooks.

"Great American Song Book" contains lyrics from Sinéad O'Connor "Troy"; Men at Work "Who Can It Be Now?"; Peter Gabriel "Shock the Monkey," "Big Time," "Digging in the Dirt"; Massive Attack "Unfinished Sympathy"; New Order "True Faith," "Bizarre Love Triangle"; Niki & The Dove "The Fox," "The Drummer"; Siouxsie and the Banshees "Cities in Dust," "Kiss Them for Me"; Björk "Hunter," "Isobel"; Depeche Mode "Everything Counts," "Strangelove," "Never Let Me Down Again," "Enjoy the Silence"; Kate Bush "Running Up That Hill (A Deal with God)," "Jig of Life"; The Cure "The Kiss"; The Fixx "One Thing Leads to Another"; The Smiths "Panic"; Yes "Owner of a Lonely Heart."

"o que você vê nelas . . ." contains a lyric from Kendrick Lamar "How Much a Dollar Cost."

"kummerspeck" is informed by a line from the poem "Philosophia Perennis" written by Anne Waldman.

"kombucha" contains the phrase "plump fine chanteuse," which comes from the documentary *Ella Fitzgerald: Just One of Those Things* (2020).

acknowledgments

Maferefun Os Aguas, meu pai Oxala, meu maes, Oxum e Yemanja Maferefun Oxchosi. Òtítóni ilé-ayé.

Wado agelisi elohi ale ageduda nvda. Wado didaneto.

In loving memory of the late Kamau Brathwaite
who taught me to claim my name.
In loving memory of the late Lucille Clifton.
In loving memory of the late Monica A. Hand.
In loving memory of the late Kathleen Fraser, who read a poem I wrote entitled "will of the estranged" & said there was a story to tell.
In loving memory of Gregory Stephen Tate. I miss you big brother.

Many of these poems-texts-proposals were written, lost, avoided, remembered, edited, salvaged, foraged, composted, in part thanks to the many residencies & funding I received over a ten-year period. Thank you Headlands, Pocantico, Image Text Ithaca, The Laundromat Project, the Sacatar Foundation, Art & History Museums - Maitland, Creative Capital, Virgina Center for the Creative Arts, Lower Manhattan Cultural Council, The George A. and Eliza Gardner Howard Foundation, The Barabara Deming Memorial Fund, Foundation for Contemporary Arts, National Endowment for the Arts, the Whiting Foundation, New York Foundation for the Arts, Millay Colony, & the Black Earth Institute.

Earlier versions of some of these poems were published in the following journals:

"it was your skin that pleased me," "taboo," "bigger," "miss moccasin," "about her," *Black Renaissance Noire,* New York University, 2008

"about her," *Poemmemoirstory* [formerly *PMS Literary Journal*], Birmingham, Alabama, 2008 "diligu wish," "asgaya aninela wish," *Black Renaissance Noire,* New York Vol. 11, Iss. 2/3, (Summer 2011)

"cliff notes" previously titled "bedside manners," *Arroyo Literary Review,* Spring, 2012

"cling", Poem-a-Day, The Academy of American Poets, June 18, 2019

To my elders.
To my second ma & my many adopted mamas.
To my prayer sisters & aunties.
To my sisters & do-or-dies.
To my dear friends & creative confidants.
To my literary & performance families.
To my former professors, who saw the very first drafts
of what would become this artifact.
My hope is that this version meets the qualifications
of what to do with a thesis project. Or not.
To the Kearney Clan. To the Obadike Clan.
To Carolyn Micklem.
To Urayoán Tomas Noel, Gabri Christa-Reid, & the Green Kimono.
To Sharifa Rhodes-Pitts & Martha Redbone.
To my editor Erika Stevens & everyone at Coffee House.

To the many who offered so much in the summer of 2006.
To the many therapists who listened, pushed tender & made me work.
To the many unnamed, w/ names, but never forgotten.
To the babies who call me Titi Tasha.
To those who are my village, wado nigada.

Coffee House Press began as a small letterpress operation in 1972 and has grown into an internationally renowned nonprofit publisher of literary fiction, essay, poetry, and other work that doesn't fit neatly into genre categories.

Coffee House is both a publisher and an arts organization. Through our *Books in Action* program and publications, we've become interdisciplinary collaborators and incubators for new work and audience experiences. Our vision for the future is one where a publisher is a catalyst and connector.

LITERATURE
is not the same thing as
PUBLISHING

Funder Acknowledgments

Coffee House Press is an internationally renowned independent book publisher and arts nonprofit based in Minneapolis, MN; through its literary publications and *Books in Action* program, Coffee House acts as a catalyst and connector—between authors and readers, ideas and resources, creativity and community, inspiration and action.

Coffee House Press books are made possible through the generous support of grants and donations from corporations, state and federal grant programs, family foundations, and the many individuals who believe in the transformational power of literature. This activity is made possible by the voters of Minnesota through a Minnesota State Arts Board Operating Support grant, thanks to the legislative appropriation from the Arts and Cultural Heritage Fund. Coffee House also receives major operating support from the Amazon Literary Partnership, Jerome Foundation, Literary Arts Emergency Fund, McKnight Foundation, and the National Endowment for the Arts (NEA). To find out more about how NEA grants impact individuals and communities, visit www.arts.gov.

Coffee House Press receives additional support from Bookmobile; Dorsey & Whitney LLP; Elmer L. & Eleanor J. Andersen Foundation; the Matching Grant Program Fund of the Minneapolis Foundation; Mr. Pancks' Fund in memory of Graham Kimpton; the Schwab Charitable Fund; and the U.S. Bank Foundation.

The Publisher's Circle of Coffee House Press

Publisher's Circle members make significant contributions to Coffee House Press's annual giving campaign. Understanding that a strong financial base is necessary for the press to meet the challenges and opportunities that arise each year, this group plays a crucial part in the success of Coffee House's mission.

Recent Publisher's Circle members include many anonymous donors, Patricia A. Beithon, Anitra Budd, Andrew Brantingham, Dave & Kelli Cloutier, Mary Ebert & Paul Stembler, Jocelyn Hale & Glenn Miller, the Rehael Fund-Roger Hale/Nor Hall of the Minneapolis Foundation, Randy Hartten & Ron Lotz, Dylan Hicks & Nina Hale, William Hardacker, Kenneth & Susan Kahn, the Kenneth Koch Literary Estate, Cinda Kornblum, Jennifer Kwon Dobbs & Stefan Liess, the Lenfestey Family Foundation, Sarah Lutman & Rob Rudolph, the Carol & Aaron Mack Charitable Fund of the Minneapolis Foundation, Gillian McCain, Mary & Malcolm McDermid, Daniel N. Smith III & Maureen Millea Smith, Enrique & Jennifer Olivarez, Robin Preble, Nan G. Swid, Grant Wood, and Margaret Wurtele.

For more information about the Publisher's Circle and other ways to support Coffee House Press books, authors, and activities, please visit www.coffeehousepress.org/pages/donate or contact us at info@coffeehousepress.org.

A writer, vocalist, and performance/ sound artist, **LaTasha N. Nevada Diggs** is the author of *TwERK* (Belladonna, 2013). Diggs has presented and performed at California Institute of the Arts, El Museo del Barrio, the Museum of Modern Art, and Walker Art Center and at festivals including Explore the North Festival, Leeuwarden, Netherlands; Hekayah Festival, Abu Dhabi; International Poetry Festival of Copenhagen; Ocean Space, Venice; International Poetry Festival of Romania; Question of Will, Slovakia; Poesiefestival, Berlin; and the 2015 Venice Biennale. As an independent curator, artistic director, and producer, Diggs has presented events for BAMcafé, Black Rock Coalition, El Museo del Barrio, the Schomburg Center for Research in Black Culture, Lincoln Center Out of Doors, and the David Rubenstein Atrium. Diggs has received a 2020 George A. and Eliza Gardner Howard Foundation Fellowship, a 2020 C.D. Wright Award for Poetry from the Foundation of Contemporary Art, a Whiting Award (2016), and a National Endowment for the Arts Literature Fellowship (2015), as well as grants and fellowships from Cave Canem, Creative Capital, New York Foundation for the Arts, and the Japan-US Friendship Commission, among others. She lives in Harlem and teaches part-time at Brooklyn College and Stetson University.

Village was designed by Bookmobile Design & Digital Publisher Services.
Text is set in Libre Baskerville Regular and Tsulehisanvhi Regular.